# "Dining out is a ritual that brings people together"

ON THE COVER: FASHION BY GIORGIO ARMANI, DINNERWARE BY MIKASA

PUBLISHERS: Richard & Cynthia Brault. CONSULTANT TO THE PUBLISHER: Richard Lavin.
EDITOR: Claudia Gioseffi. ART & PRODUCTION DIRECTOR: Paul Dushkind.
RESTAURANT CORRESPONDENT: Richard Martini. PHOTOGRAPHERS: Martin Cohen, Kingmond Young.
DESIGN CONSULTANT: Matt Foster. ASSOCIATE PUBLISHER: Mark Schwarz.
SALES & MARKETING MANAGER: Tracy Tooker-Griswold. ADMINISTRATIVE OFFICER & FINANCIAL DIRECTOR:
Paula Neuhardt Mayer. CONTROLLER: Nestor Babula. ASSISTANT TO THE CONTROLLER: Djaja Hardjadinata.
OFFICE ASSISTANT: Melanie Pauly.

Epicurean Rendezvous is published by Epicurean Rendezvous, Inc.,
75 Howell Avenue, Larchmont, NY 10538 • TEL: 914-833-2676 FAX: 914-833-0333
Copyright © 1993. NO REPRODUCTION OF THIS MAGAZINE IN WHOLE OR IN PART IS ALLOWED
WITHOUT EXPRESS PERMISSION OF THE PUBLISHER.
PRINTED IN KOREA / CODRA: 310.212.7155

ISBN 0-933875-26-6

# CONTENTS

◆

## ◆ RESTAURANTS ◆

## ◆ *world-class wines* ◆

BY NORMAN ROBY

## ◆ *the best of cigars* ◆

BY RICHARD L. DI MEOLA

## ◆ *symbols* ◆

VISA WELCOMED_____ **VISA**

RESERVATIONS ACCEPTED _____ ☎ 💌 ____JACKET AND TIE REQUIRED

FULL BAR_____ 🍸 🎵 ____LIVE ENTERTAINMENT

VALET PARKING _____ 🚗 PR _____PRIVATE ROOM

VIEW _____ 📷 ✦ _____OUTDOOR DINING

ROMANTIC_____ 👥 ♡ ____HEALTH-CONSCIOUS MENU

LIVELY_____ 😊 ∅ ____NO SMOKING ANYWHERE

Perfectly balanced.

Tanqueray®

# THE
# EPICUREAN RENDEZVOUS
# AND VISA
# FREQUENT DINING
# & GIVING PROGRAM

**THE GIVING PROGRAM**

Epicurean Rendezvous restaurants have traditionally been major supporters of charities. These include New York Citymeals-on-Wheels, Meals on Wheels America, Share our Strength, The March of Dimes and other important national and local charitable organizations. Restaurants contribute to the charities in many ways such as, monetary donations, gift certificates for benefit events, catering services and food donations. The principals of the Epicurean Rendezvous restaurants have also contributed many hours of their personal time, organizing events on behalf of the charities and making personal appearances at various events and galas. These Epicurean Rendezvous restaurants set the highest example of hospitality and generosity of spirit in the industry.

This year, nearly 800 great chefs and restaurateurs, Visa, Epicurean Rendezvous, Club Med and The Brands that Care have joined forces to raise money for Meals on Wheels. All the monies are being donated in the name of the participating and supporting Epicurean Rendezvous restaurants, and 100% of the monies raised go to the charities. These restaurants are identified on their editorial page by this legend: FREQUENT DINING & GIVING PROGRAM.

Every time you pay the check with a Visa Card, every time you ask for a free copy of the Epicurean Rendezvous Guide and every time you order the Brands That Care in the participating restaurants, a donation from Epicurean Rendezvous or Visa will be made to your local Meals on Wheels care providers.

**THE CHARITY**

Meals on Wheels care providers deliver hot meals and emergency meals to the homebound elderly.

Thousands of homebound elderly persons in communities throughout America receive five hot meals a week, which are underwritten by government funds administered by various local care providers. Funds from the Epicurean Rendezvous Frequent Dining & Giving Program are given to the local care

# How to be accepted by your colleagues, your clients and, most important, your waiter.

Somewhere along the line, a business card came to be viewed as something of a personal statement.

Fair enough. But at Visa, we've always felt that the most impressive statement a card can make is "I'll pay for this."

Accordingly, no card is accepted at more places than the Visa® Business Card: over 10 million worldwide. That's over 6 million more than American Express.

And by the way, if you really want to raise some eyebrows, try using an American Express card in one of the many restaurants that no longer take it.

The Visa Business Card can make you look good in a lot of other ways, too. It gives you access to cash advances at more than 410,000 locations. It offers you customized, neatly summarized reports of your spending by date and category. And it provides you with the convenience of flexible spending and billing options.

So if you believe that performance is the truest mark of prestige, look into the Visa Business Card.

You won't just be respected wherever you go. You'll be accepted wherever you go.

**VISA**

providers to ensure that our neighborhood's aged shut-ins are not forced to go without meals on weekends, holidays, or in emergencies. In 1981, in New York City, a unique partnering of private donations and government funds started the complimentary delivery of meals to the homebound elderly on weekends and holidays. Since then, many other Meals on Wheels local care providers around the country have emulated this successful partnering.

The Epicurean Rendezvous Board of Advisors, with guidance from prominent leaders among the Meals On Wheels care providers, will help determine the distribution of funds. One hundred percent of all funds raised in the Giving and Brands that Care programs will go to Meals On Wheels.

**THE EPICUREAN RENDEZVOUS BOOK**  Epicurean Rendezvous is the most comprehensive and reliable guide to fine dining in America. It contains 200 pages of colorful photos and editorial celebrating the talent behind the best restaurants in New York, Southern California, Northern California and Florida. Every time you dine at a participating restaurant and pay with your Visa card, just ask for a free copy of the guidebook, any edition (one per party).

**THE FREQUENT DINING PROGRAM**  Every time you dine at one of Epicurean Rendezvous's participating restaurants between November 1993 and November 1994, use Visa to pay for your meal (either breakfast, lunch or dinner) and earn two points. If you pay with any other card, you earn one point. The minimum purchase amount per meal is $50, including tax and tip. When you earn 50 points you will receive a $100 gift certificate for use at a participating Epicurean Rendezvous restaurant.

**400 CLUB MED AWARDS FOR TWO**  Club Med is the original all-encompassing, all-inclusive resort. The Club Med villages are unique, memorable and definitely out of the ordinary.

Anybody is eligible for a one-week Club Med vacation for two (North American destinations, land only). Simply come up with your own idea for raising more money for Meals on Wheels and write an essay about it in 50 words or less. Entries will be evaluated by a carefully selected panel and the 400 best respondents will be awarded a Club Med vacation for two.

With 17 North American villages, Club Med has been welcoming vacationers to their luxurious resorts since 1968. Call 1-800-CLUB MED for a brochure.

**THE PLEDGE**  Epicurean Rendezvous has pledged a minimum $100,000 to the charities against twenty cents a copy of every Epicurean Rendezvous Guide given to a guest, in every participating restaurant for a year.

# DELTA'S NEW NORTH AMERICAN FIRST CLASS SERVICE

DELTA FIRST

## Now You Don't Have To Travel Around The World For Fine Dining.

With a wide selection of healthy, contemporary meals, prepared daily from the freshest ingredients, Delta offers a new, unsurpassed North American First Class Service, featuring wines selected by Anthony Dias Blue. From Delta, we wish you bon voyage and bon appetit. Call your Travel Agent or Delta at 1-800-221-1212.

## ▲ DELTA AIR LINES

Visa has pledged a minimum $100,000 to the charities against five cents a transaction for every transaction, in every participating restaurant, every day for a year.

The Brands That Care will help raise additional funds for the Meals on Wheels care providers. Epicurean Rendezvous will give $1 per bottle to the charities based on product consumed in the participating Epicurean Rendezvous restaurants. Up to ten percent of the brand's advertising expenditures will be donated by Epicurean Rendezvous on behalf of the restaurants.

**FREQUENT DINING RULES**

EARNING POINTS & PRIZES: Every time you dine at a participating Epicurean Rendezvous restaurant between November 5, 1993 and October 31, 1994, you may earn Frequent Dining points. The participating restaurants are identified on their editorial page in the latest Epicurean Rendezvous guide by this legend: FREQUENT DINING & GIVING PROGRAM. The participating restaurants are also listed in the Epicurean Rendezvous brochure. Pay with any payment card and earn one point. Pay with a Visa card and earn two points. Point(s) are earned per transaction with a minimum $50 purchase including tax and tip. You may earn point(s) no more than once per day in the same restaurant, and no more than half (25) of your points may come from the same restaurant.

TRACKING POINTS: Track your own points by collecting payment card receipts from your transactions at participating restaurants. On your receipts blacken on the front and back (or cut out) all digits of your card number except the first six digits. Only payment card receipts qualify for points. Combinations of payment card receipts are acceptable if in the name of the same person. You may submit your receipts (or legible photocopies) only when 50 points are accumulated. Send them with your complete name and address to: Epicurean Rendezvous Frequent Dining Program, P. O. Box 371855, Omaha, NE 68137-8055. All claims must be received by December 1, 1994.

Claims are subject to verification by an independent judging organization whose decisions are final. No responsibility is assumed for lost, late or misdirected mail. Late requests cannot be honored. Offer void where prohibited, taxed, or otherwise restricted by law. Open to New York, New Jersey, Connecticut, Pennsylvania, California and Florida residents only. Epicurean Rendezvous reserves the right to nullify any claims which it believes are forged or cannot be substantiated. An explanation will be provided within 30 days. You may correct

**The French** call it *"joie de vivre".* A joyous celebration of **life's** unexpected moments. Moments meant for B&B. **With a** taste derived from a mysterious combination of **exotic** spices, B&B excites the palate and delights the **imagination.** Discover it straight up or over ice.

To send a gift of B&B, where legal, call 1-800-238-4373

or replace the disputed transactions and re-submit your claim. Sponsors reserve the right to amend the rules or cancel this promotion at any time without prior notice. By participating, you have granted Epicurean Rendezvous the right to provide your name and address to its participating restaurants, unless written notification otherwise is submitted with your claim.

GIFT CERTIFICATES: Accumulate 50 points and you are eligible to receive a $100 gift certificate to an Epicurean Rendezvous restaurant in your region. Your restaurant gift certificate is redeemable for $100 value in food and beverages (subject to local laws and excluding tax and gratuities) only at the issuing restaurant. It will be issued within 30 days of submitting statements for validation. Gift certificates are not redeemable for cash or credit and may be subject to availability of reservations and other restrictions. They are issued by region, in alphabetical rotation by restaurant name, and are valid for 90 days. No cash or credit refund on unused portion.

**CLUB MED AWARDS RULES**

To enter the "Epicurean Rendezvous Club Med Awards Contest," describe your idea for raising money to help feed the homebound elderly in 50 words or less. You may include your contest entry with your Frequent Dining gift certificate claim. Or you can mail contest entry directly to the sponsor at the following address: Epicurean Rendezvous Contest, 75 Howell Avenue, Larchmont, NY 10538. Type or clearly print your idea and include your name, complete address and social security number (necessary for tax purposes only, in the event you are a winner). Purchase not required to enter. Limit: one entry per household.

Contest begins November 5, 1993. Entries must be received by December 1, 1994. No illegible or incomplete entries accepted. No responsibility is assumed for lost, misdirected, mutilated, postage due or late entries. Entries become exclusive property of sponsor and will not be returned.

Entry submissions must be original, never before published or adapted from previously published material and may in no way infringe upon any copyrighted or trademarked material. Entries will be judged on the following criteria: creativity (15%), originality (15%), appropriateness to contest theme (30%) and practicality of exercising the idea successfully (40%). In the event of a tie, the essay with the highest score for practicality of executing the idea successfully will win. Judging will be conducted by Epicurean Rendezvous under guidelines established by an independent judging organization. Judges' decisions are final.

Club Med Resort Vacations will be awarded to the 400 contestants with the highest scores. Each vacation is for two and includes 7 days/6 nights double occupancy accommodations and meals at winner's choice of a North American Club Med destination, subject to availability as determined at the sole discretion of Club Med Sales, Inc. Round-trip airfare, transfers, taxes, gratuities and other expenses not covered herein are not included. Estimated value of each trip for two: $2,000. Total estimated value of all prizes: $800,000. Prizes are not transferable or redeemable for cash. Blackout dates and advance booking requirements apply. All travel must be completed by July 31, 1995. A minor must be accompanied by an adult. All prizes will be awarded provided a sufficient quantity of eligible entries (as determined by the independent judging organization) are received. No duplicate prize winners or substitution for prizes. Winners will be notified by mail on or before February 28, 1995. Epicurean Rendezvous and Club Med Sales, Inc. assume no liability in connection with the acceptance, operation or use of the prizes awarded. Epicurean Rendezvous makes no express warranty, guaranty or representation of any kind concerning prizes, and disclaims any implied guaranties. Winners, upon accepting their prizes, agree to all terms and conditions detailed in the official contest rules and in Club Med Sales, Inc. materials provided to the winners.

All taxes are the responsibility of winners. Winners may be required to execute an affidavit of eligibility/release of liability, statement of originality, travel companion release and grant any and all publication rights to sponsor within 14 days of date printed on notification, or prize may be awarded to an alternate winner.

All essays and all rights to their publication become the property of Epicurean Rendezvous which may use, edit and excerpt these entries for promotional or any other purpose without attribution or further compensation. Epicurean Rendezvous and its affiliates reserve the right to use prize winners' names, hometown and likenesses in any promotional activities relating to this contest without further notification, permission, or compensation to the winners, except where prohibited by law.

Contest is open to all legal residents of New York, New Jersey, Connecticut, Pennsylvania, California and Florida, aged 18 and older. Employees of Epicurean Rendezvous, Club Med Sales, Inc., Visa U.S.A., Inc. and Visa International Service Association, their affiliates, subsidiaries, distributors, advertising and promotional agencies, other agents, judges and their immediate families, are not eligible. Subject to all federal, state and local laws and regulations. VOID WHERE PROHIBITED OR RESTRICTED BY LAW.

For the names of winners, send a stamped, self-addressed envelope to be received by December 1, 1994, to: Trip Winners, P. O. Box 371856, Omaha, NE 68137-8056.

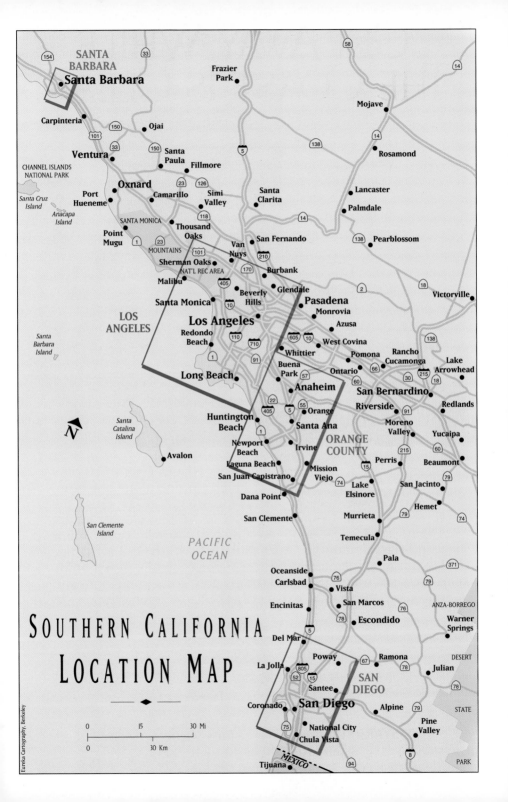

SANTA
BARBARA
**Santa Barbara**

(154) (33)

Frazier
Park

(58)

(14)

Mojave

Carpinteria

(150) Ojai

(101) (33) (150) Santa
Paula

**Ventura** Fillmore

(138) Rosamond

(14)

Santa
Clarita

Lancaster

Palmdale

CHANNEL ISLANDS
NATIONAL PARK

Santa Cruz
Island

Anacapa
Island

**Oxnard** (23) (126) Simi
Valley
Port
Hueneme Camarillo

SANTA MONICA Thousand
Oaks

Point
Mugu (1)

(23)

MOUNTAINS (101)

Sherman Oaks

NAT'L REC AREA

Malibu

Van
Nuys

San Fernando

(138) Pearblossom

(14)

(405)

(170) Burbank

Beverly Glendale
Hills

(2)

(18)

Victorville

**LOS
ANGELES**

Santa Monica

(10)

**Pasadena**
Monrovia

Azusa

**Los Angeles**
Redondo
Beach

(110) (710)

(605) (10) West Covina

Rancho
Cucamonga

(138)

Santa
Barbara
Island

(1)

(91)

Whittier
Buena
Park (57)

Pomona

Ontario

(66)

(30) (215)

Lake
Arrowhead

(18)

**Long Beach**

**Anaheim**

(60)

**San Bernardino**

Santa
Catalina
Island

(22)
(405) (5)

(55) Orange

Riverside

(91)

Redlands

Moreno
Valley

Yucaipa

Avalon

**Huntington
Beach**

(1)

Santa Ana

**ORANGE
COUNTY**

(215)

(60)

Beaumont

Newport
Beach

Irvine

Perris

Laguna Beach

Mission
Viejo (74)

Lake
Elsinore

San Jacinto

Hemet

San Juan Capistrano

(79)

(74)

Dana Point

Murrieta

(79)

San Clemente

*Santa
Barbara
Island*

*San Clemente
Island*

Temecula

Pala

(371)

*PACIFIC
OCEAN*

Oceanside
Carlsbad

(76)

(79)

Vista

Encinitas

San Marcos

(76)

ANZA-BORREGO

(78) Escondido

Warner
Springs

# SOUTHERN CALIFORNIA

Del Mar

(5)

DESERT

# LOCATION MAP

La Jolla

(805)

Poway

(52) (15)

(67) Ramona

(78)

Julian

(78)

**SAN
DIEGO**

Santee

Coronado

**San Diego**

Alpine

(79)

STATE

(75)

**National City**

Pine
Valley

Chula Vista

*Eureka Cartography, Berkeley*

0        15        30 Mi

0              30 Km

MEXICO

Tijuana

(94)

(8)

PARK

N

# GET AWAY WHILE THE COAST IS CLEAR.

Come visit The Ritz-Carlton, Laguna Niguel, California's only Five-Star, Five-Diamond resort hotel. Unwind along our beautiful, uncrowded beach. Join us for Afternoon Tea. Enjoy the sunset from our ocean-front lounge or our new Ocean Terrace. Then start off a romantic evening with dinner at one of our world-class restaurants. After dinner, the Club Grill is the perfect place for dancing and late night cocktails. You'll enjoy tennis, golf, water sports and the gracious accommodations and uncompromising service that only The Ritz-Carlton can provide.

### THE RITZ-CARLTON
#### LAGUNA NIGUEL

33533 Ritz-Carlton Drive, Laguna Niguel, CA 92677
714/240-2000 or 800/241-3333

one of *The Leading Hotels of the World*®

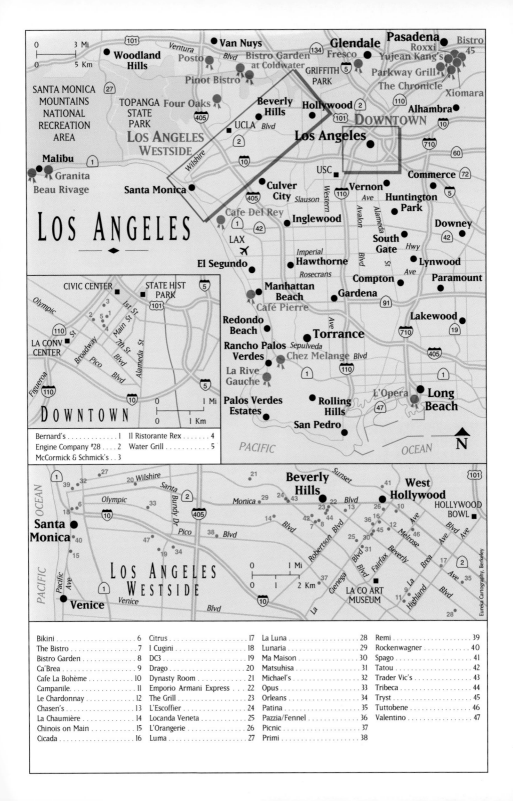

# LOS ANGELES

**Main map labels:**

101 Ventura Blvd — Van Nuys — 134 Glendale — Pasadena — Bistro 45 — Roxxi

Woodland Hills — Posto — Bistro Garden at Coldwater — Fresco — Yujean Kang's — Parkway Grill — The Chronicle

Pinot Bistro — GRIFFITH PARK — 5 — Xiomara

SANTA MONICA MOUNTAINS NATIONAL RECREATION AREA — 27 — TOPANGA STATE PARK — Four Oaks — 405 — Beverly Hills — Hollywood — 2 — 110 — Alhambra

UCLA Blvd — 101 — DOWNTOWN — 10

LOS ANGELES WESTSIDE — 2 — Los Angeles — 710

Malibu — 1 — 60

Granita — Wilshire — 10 — 90

Beau Rivage — USC — Vernon — Commerce — 72

Santa Monica — 405 — Culver City — Slauson — 110 — Huntington Park — 5

Cafe Del Rey — 1 — Inglewood — Avalon — Downey — 42

LAX — 42 — South Gate — Hwy

El Segundo — Hawthorne — Lynwood

Imperial — Rosecrans — Compton — Paramount

Manhattan Beach — Gardena — 91 — Lakewood

Café Pierre — 710 — 19

Redondo Beach — Torrance — 405

Rancho Palos Verdes — Sepulveda — Chez Melange — Blvd — 1

La Rive Gauche — 1 — 110 — 1

Palos Verdes Estates — Rolling Hills — L'Opera — Long Beach — 47

San Pedro — **N**

PACIFIC — OCEAN

## DOWNTOWN

CIVIC CENTER — STATE HIST PARK — 5

Olympic — 1st St — 101

LA CONV CENTER — 110 — Main St — 7th St — Alameda St

Broadway — Pico — Blvd

Figueroa — 110 — 10 — 5

0 — 1 Mi / 0 — 1 Km

## LOS ANGELES WESTSIDE

OCEAN — Wilshire — Santa Monica — 101

Olympic — Bundy Dr — 405 — Beverly Hills — West Hollywood — HOLLYWOOD BOWL

Santa Monica — Pico — Blvd — Robertson Blvd — Melrose — Beverly — Brea — La — Highland

Venice — Venice Blvd — 10

LA CO ART MUSEUM

0 — 1 Mi / 0 — 1 — 2 Km

Eureka Cartography, Berkeley

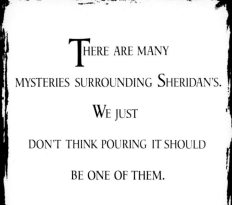

THERE ARE MANY

MYSTERIES SURROUNDING SHERIDAN'S.

WE JUST

DON'T THINK POURING IT SHOULD

BE ONE OF THEM.

*First pour the black over ice.*

*Next float the white.*

Patent Pending

SHERIDAN'S.™ A STUNNING PERFORMANCE IN BLACK AND WHITE.

# BERNARD'S

THE BILTMORE HOTEL
500 SOUTH GRAND AVENUE
LOS ANGELES, CA 90071
(213) 612-1580
*Visa & Major Credit Cards*
*Dinner Mon–Sat • Lunch Mon–Fri*

*Director of Food & Beverage*
ERNESTO BRANDNER

*Chef de Cuisine*
PHILIPPE TROSCH
*Executive Chef*
ROGER PIGOZZI

## Menu Highlights
❦

*Appetizers*
NORWEGIAN SALMON GRAVLAX,
BARLEY & HERB RISOTTO, SPICY
CUCUMBER SALAD • KENTUCKY
LIMESTONE LETTUCE,
SWEET ONION, TOMATOES,
CHOPPED WALNUTS &
CRUMPLED ROQUEFORT

*Entrées*
BAKED PETRALE SOLE &
DUNGENESS CRAB, YELLOW
TOMATO & ASPARAGUS SAUCE
• ROASTED CHILEAN SEABASS,
EGGPLANT & ORGANIC TOMATO
CRUST

A STEP INTO THE BILTMORE HOTEL IS A STEP INTO A PIECE OF LOS Angeles history. Since 1923, the grand hotel has been the centerpiece of Pershing Square, while the hotel's heart for the past seven years has been Bernard's, with its elegant high wooden ceilings and refined cuisine. ♦ Executive Chef Roger Pigozzi took the classical French cuisine Bernard's was famous for and added some California imagination. The region's abundance of fresh vegetables and fish complements his traditional approach nicely. Atlantic salmon, sliced fresh at the table, special oysters, notable for their variety and flavor and flown in from the Pacific Northwest, and risotto with wild forest mushrooms are standout dishes. Occasionally osso buco and New York steak appear among the specialties. For dessert, Bernard's famous Black Plate is prerequisite to sampling the chef's other delectable chocolate endings.

**AVERAGE DINNER FOR TWO: $80**
DOES NOT INCLUDE WINE, TAX AND GRATUITY

**MEDITERRANEAN**
FREQUENT DINING & GIVING PROGRAM

# BEAU RIVAGE

26025 PACIFIC COAST HIGHWAY
MALIBU, CA 90265
(310) 456-5733

*Visa & Major Credit Cards*
*Open Daily • Dinner Only • Sunday Brunch*

*Proprietors*
DANIEL &
LUCIANA FORGE

*Chef*
ANDREAS KISLER

## Menu Highlights

*Appetizers*
SNAILS IN PHYLLO PURSE
• GAZPACHO NEPTUNE:
CLAM BROTH, SCALLIONS,
AVOCADO, TOMATO,
CUCUMBER & BAY SHRIMP

*Entrées*
LINGUINI POLLO WITH
MUSHROOMS • FILET OF
WILD BOAR WITH
CHESTNUTS • BRANZINO
BASS, MACADEMIAS, SWEET
RED ONIONS, PESTO
IN GRAPE LEAF

AFTER FORTY YEARS IN THE RESTAURANT BUSINESS, FOURTEEN AS owners of the successful L'Auberge in Hollywood, Daniel and Luciana Forge were ready to retire. They bought a beautiful piece of land in Malibu and split their time between California and Nice, France. But the Forges couldn't resist the lure of the restaurant business, and in 1982, they remodeled an old building on their property and opened Beau Rivage. ♦ Inspired by the South of France's elegant country inns, the restaurant has a tile roof, walls covered with vines, and abundant flower and herb gardens that supply the kitchen. There are six dining areas: a glass hall overlooking the ocean, a dining room warmed by wood and high ceiling beams, an enclosed garden patio with a small fountain, and a wine cellar that seats twelve. ♦ All provide a perfect backdrop for Chef Andreas Kisler's Mediterranean cuisine, with its emphasis on French and Italian seafood, pasta, meat and game dishes, and Pastry Chef Genevieve Boyer's fabulous desserts, including praline *feuilletés*. Popular for weddings and private parties, Beau Rivage can accommodate up to 250 guests.

**AVERAGE DINNER FOR TWO: $70**
DOES NOT INCLUDE WINE, TAX AND GRATUITY

# THE BISTRO

246 NORTH CAÑON DRIVE
BEVERLY HILLS, CA 90210
(310) 273-5633

*Visa & Major Credit Cards*
*Dinner Mon-Sat*

| Proprietors | Chef |
|---|---|
| KURT NIKLAS | GILLES DIRAT |
| CHRISTOPHER NIKLAS | |

## Menu Highlights

*Appetizers*
ESCARGOTS BOURGUIGNON
• PISTOU SOUP
• RISOTTO WITH LOBSTER & ASPARAGUS

*Entrées*
SEARED SCALLOPS
WITH CAVIAR CREAM
• GRILLED LAMB CHOPS
WITH PORT ROSEMARY SAUCE
• BROILED SHRIMPS
WITH MUSTARD SAUCE

CELEBRATING ITS THIRTIETH ANNIVERSARY, THE BISTRO IS A neighborhood fixture in Beverly Hills. Opened in 1963 by Kurt Niklas as a successor to Romanoff's (a fabulous gathering place for Hollywood royalty), his elegant restaurant went beyond the modest bistro he intended. The dining room is lavishly decorated in turn-of-the-century Parisian style, with hand-painted structural columns and extravagantly etched glass that return you to a bygone era of glamour. ◆ The French-Continental cuisine is unpretentious and reliably good. The dishes that young and talented Chef Gilles Dirat keeps alive and thriving are classic favorites many other places have forgotten. His desserts, such as a cloudlike chocolate soufflé, are easily remembered. Formerly of Le Périgord in New York, Dirat's lighter offerings complement the regular menu. ◆ An establishment with a loyal and cohesive staff, The Bistro is able to accommodate from thirty to 300 in its private party facilities.

**AVERAGE DINNER FOR TWO: $55**
DOES NOT INCLUDE WINE, TAX AND GRATUITY

# BISTRO 45

45 SOUTH MENTOR AVENUE
NEAR LAKE & COLORADO
PASADENA, CA 91106
(818) 795-2478

*Visa & Major Credit Cards*
*Dinner Tues-Sun • Lunch Tues-Fri*

*Proprietor*
ROBERT SIMON

*Chef*
SEAN SHERIDAN

## Menu Highlights

*Appetizers*
NORWEGIAN SALMON
& AHI TARTARE
• SAUTÉED FRESH CALAMARI

*Entrées*
GRILLED VIRGINIA SEA
SCALLOPS WITH CUMIN
ROASTED VEGETABLES & BEETS
À LA JULIENNE • CASSOULET
• BOUILLABAISSE FOR TWO
• PAN-ROASTED NEW ZEALAND
ELK WITH GARLIC SAUCE

PASADENA HAS SOMETHING NEW, INNOVATIVE AND SOPHISTI-cated going for it — Bistro 45. Veteran restaurateur Robert Simon, for-mer owner of Cafe Jacoulet in Old Town Pasadena, has polished his resume with a bistro that sizzles. "With an amazing ability to remember names, he's at every table making things happen," says his manager. ♦ Visually, the bistro is a mix of verticals. Tall bar, thin front door and nar-row latticed porch counterpoint pale peach walls with copper sconces shaped like ice cream cones. Tempered glass windows give the divided dining rooms an underwater softness, and large abstract paintings pro-vide splashes of color. ♦ Monthly French, Italian and California wine-maker dinners emphasize the restaurant's commitment to serious dining, and Chef Sean Sheridan articulates the pleasantly varied French/California menu with fashionable, yet classical verve. The City of Roses definitely has another flower in its bonnet.

**AVERAGE DINNER FOR TWO: $48**
DOES NOT INCLUDE WINE, TAX & GRATUITY

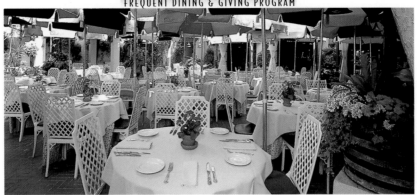

**CONTINENTAL**
FREQUENT DINING & GIVING PROGRAM

# THE BISTRO GARDEN

176 NORTH CAÑON DRIVE
BEVERLY HILLS, CA 90210
(310) 550-3900

*Visa & Major Credit Cards*
*Lunch & Dinner Mon-Sat*

| *Proprietors* | *Chef* |
|---|---|
| CHRISTOPHER NIKLAS | HARRY KLIBINGAT |
| KURT NIKLAS | |

## Menu Highlights

*Appetizers*
HOUSE-CURED SALMON
WITH DILL SAUCE
• DUNGENESS CRAB
ON ICE

*Entrées*
BROILED
LAKE SUPERIOR
WHITE FISH
• FRESH AHI,
CAJUN STYLE
• OSSO BUCCO
WITH SAFFRON
• SWISS BRATWURST

DESPITE ITS CHIC CLIENTELE, THE BISTRO GARDEN IS DELIGHTFULLY unintimidating. The famous Bistro's enchanting offspring, it is L.A.'s premier garden restaurant. A fountain, festive umbrellas, pastel tablecloths and lattice-back chairs create a fantasy mood for lunch or dinner. In this setting, a late supper of fluffy soufflés and Champagne becomes almost magical when accompanied by music from a grand piano. ♦ Owners Kurt and Christopher Niklas strive daily to please all their customers, famous or not. "It's the people who come here who really make the place," says Kurt. Another crowd-pleaser is Chef Harry Klibingat, who brings his lightened version of Continental cuisine to the Bistro tradition of healthy dining. ♦ With its relaxed California style and its storybook charm, The Bistro Garden is a natural choice for celebrations. Both the garden and the spacious private room, which accommodates up to 250 guests, are always in demand for Sunday weddings, special galas and media events.

**AVERAGE DINNER FOR TWO: $50**
DOES NOT INCLUDE WINE, TAX AND GRATUITY

# BIKINI

1413 FIFTH STREET
SANTA MONICA, CA 90401
(310) 395-8611
*Visa & Major Credit Cards*
*Dinner Mon-Sat • Lunch Tues-Sat*

*General Manager*
ANDREW NAKANO

*Chef/Proprietor*
JOHN SEDLAR
*Chef*
ROBERT SIMMELINK

## Menu Highlights

*Appetizers*
SCRAMBLED DUCK EGGS WITH
GINGERED DUCK CONFIT &
WATER CHESTNUTS IN DUCK
SHELLS • TUNA SASHIMI
PLATE WITH CAVIAR

*Entrées*
ROASTED BREAST OF
CHICKEN WITH PEANUT
SAUCE & RICE NOODLES
• GRILLED SADDLE OF LAMB
WITH INDIAN SPICES &
GREEN CURRY SAUCE
• SALMON WITH BABY
VEGETABLE CHOP SUEY,
WASABI & PLUM SAUCES

BIKINI IS A GOOD NAME FOR A LOS ANGELES RESTAURANT
that has made one of the biggest splashes in recent years. As you sit down
amid the action in the main room with its stunning two-story windows,
brace yourself for a heightened level of dining. The mezzanine overlooks
the room below, and plush private booths are lulled by the quiet roar of
Eric Orr's waterfall. The restaurant's ornate bar faces an open-to-the-sky
courtyard. ◆ John Sedlar keeps the excitement going on the plate,
whether there's food on it or not. A stickler for presentation, he designed
his own collection, including the much-talked-about "Madonna" plate
(the original version). Sedlar also travels the world for menu ideas. From
South American comes his "Nacatamal," or tropical TV dinner, an
extraordinary appetizer based on plaintains, from Sante Fe his tamale bar,
*twelve* different takes on the classic. From Russia come the magnificent
eggs Fabergé, a dessert made with white and dark chocolate eggshells filled
with tangerine mousse. ◆ Guests can top off an evening with Cognac and
a cigar on the courtyard.

**AVERAGE DINNER FOR TWO: $65**
DOES NOT INCLUDE WINE, TAX AND GRATUITY

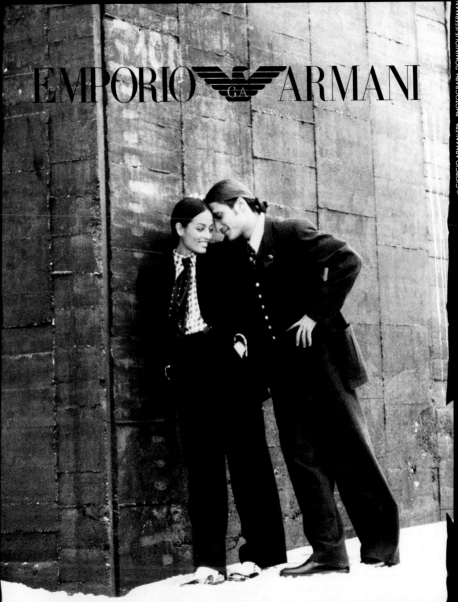

# EMPORIO ARMANI

# Stoli® Cristall.
### The World's Rarest Vodka.

# THE BISTRO GARDEN AT COLDWATER

12950 VENTURA BOULEVARD
STUDIO CITY, CA 91604
(818) 501-0202

*Visa & Major Credit Cards*
*Open Daily For Dinner • Lunch Mon-Fri*

| Proprietor | Chef |
|---|---|
| CHRISTOPHER NIKLAS | FRANÇOIS MEULIEN |

## Menu Highlights

*Appetizers*

JUMBO
CRAB SALAD
• FRESH
OYSTERS
• GRILLED
SHRIMP SALAD,
SPICY WILD RICE

*Entrées*

COQ AU VIN
• AIOLI
• PEPPER STEAK

LOCATED IN THE SAN FERNANDO VALLEY, THE BISTRO GARDEN at Coldwater is the latest collaboration of restaurant pioneer Kurt Niklas and his son Christopher. On the other side of Beverly Hills, the duo's original Bistro and their Bistro Garden have become institutions, and their new venture is a success as well. Residents of the relatively untapped culinary region no longer need to spend hours on the freeway in search of a good meal. Equally appreciative are studio people from nearby NBC, Universal and Columbia Pictures who now have a high-profile eatery for power lunches in the Valley. ♦ "Clientele is ambiance," says proprietor Christopher Niklas. Meals at The Bistro Garden are often star-studded entertainment for those who like to people-watch. True to its bistro and brasserie roots, the restaurant offers light fare in a boisterous atmosphere. Hearty country French dishes, such as broiled shrimp with mustard sauce and cassoulet Toulousain, are served in the restaurant's sun-dappled, glass-enclosed winter garden with its spectacular thirty-foot ceiling.

**AVERAGE DINNER FOR TWO: $45**
DOES NOT INCLUDE WINE, TAX AND GRATUITY

# CA'BREA

346 SOUTH LA BREA AVE.
AT THIRD STREET
LOS ANGELES, CA 90036
(213) 938-2863
*Visa & Major Credit Cards*
*Dinner Mon–Sat • Lunch Mon–Fri*

*Co-Proprietor*
THOMAS SWEET

*Chef/Proprietor*
ANTONIO TOMASSI

## Menu Highlights

*Appetizers*

SAUTÉED SHRIMP & CRABCAKES
WITH AN ONION CONFIT • GOAT
CHEESE WRAPPED IN PANCETTA,
BAKED ON A BED OF SPINACH
• FRESH SEAFOOD WITH
MARINATED VEGETABLES IN
A LEMON & GARLIC DRESSING

*Entrées*

HOUSEMADE VENETIAN PASTA
WITH LOBSTER, CLAMS, SCAL-
LOPS, SHRIMP & PORCINI
• ROASTED DUCK IN HONEY-BAL-
SAMIC SAUCE • BROILED WHOLE
BONELESS CHICKEN, MARINATED
IN WINE, HERBS & SPICES

"THERE ARE THREE GREAT PLEASURES IN LIFE," SAY CO-PROPRI-
etor Jean-Louis De Mori, "sleeping, making love and appreciating good
food." It seems De Mori's philosophy was influenced by Venetian parents
and formative years in Paris. Later, a move to Florence was personally for-
tuitous. There he met the American woman who would become his wife,
leading to their migration to her native Los Angeles. Notoriety came
when he joined Antonio Tomassi of Orsini's and Rex fame to create their
highly successful Locanda Veneta. ♦ Now the charismatic partners are on
another culinary journey called Ca'Brea. Tomassi outdoes himself with a
panoply of Italian delicacies, giving special attention to risottos and *frutti
di mare.* Named "Best Dish" by *Esquire,* his medley of Italian beans with
sage and babyback ribs, alone, is worth the drive. ♦ Florentine architect
Andre Benaim gives the restaurant romance with intimate lighting, an
opulent marble bar and cathedral ceilings. Diners are encouraged to linger
over a meal. As Co-Proprietor Tom Sweet puts it, "Dining in Los Angeles
was once only part of an evening, here at Ca'Brea, it *is* the evening."

**AVERAGE DINNER FOR TWO: $45**
DOES NOT INCLUDE WINE, TAX AND GRATUITY

CALIFORNIA
FREQUENT DINING & GIVING PROGRAM

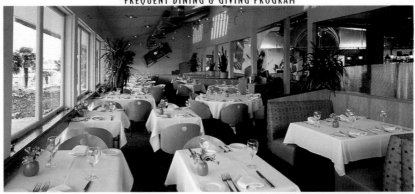

# CAFE DEL REY

4451 ADMIRALTY WAY
AT BALI WAY
MARINA DEL REY, CA 90292
(310) 823-6395
*Visa & Major Credit Cards*
*Open Daily for Dinner • Lunch Mon-Sat • Sunday Brunch*

| *General Manager* | *Chef* |
|---|---|
| STEVE WUEBBENS | KATSUO NAGASAWA |

## Menu Highlights

*Appetizers*

GRILLED RABBIT WITH WILD
MUSHROOMS & SWEET ONION
SAUCE IN FILO CUP • SASHIMI
SALAD WITH CRISPY NOODLES,
CUCUMBER SPAGHETTI &
YUZU DRESSING

*Entrées*

AIR-DRIED PEKING DUCK,
MANGO CHUTNEY, RICE
TORTILLAS, HERBED VEGETABLES,
GOLDEN RAISINS & PLUM WINE
SAUCE • ROASTED HALIBUT,
LOBSTER, SCALLOP & SHRIMP
GLACAGE, STIR FRY VEGETABLES
& SAFFRON TOMATO SAUCE

AS ITS NAME IMPLIES, DINING IN CAFE DEL REY IS LIKE BEING served aboard one of the elegant yachts docked at Marina del Rey. Boats of every size and color bob on the water outside the restaurant, while the sumptuous interior design captures the innovative lighting and elegant woods of a luxury seacraft. ♦ General Manager Stephen Wuebbens maintains Cafe Del Rey's extensive California wine list, the selections in perfect harmony with the eclectic menu. Chef Katsuo Nagasawa, formerly of Bistango, blends a spectrum of flavors from outside California's borders, including Asian and Southwestern influences. The uniquely prepared fresh fish on the menu, including seared ahi, pan-fried sand dabs, grilled pesto salmon and Thai shellfish sausage, is particularly noteworthy. Although twenty percent of the restaurant's dishes change daily, the view of the Marina from this romantic hideaway is timeless.

**AVERAGE DINNER FOR TWO: $64**
DOES NOT INCLUDE WINE, TAX AND GRATUITY

# CAFÉ PIERRE

317 MANHATTAN BEACH BOULEVARD
MANHATTAN BEACH, CA 90266
(310) 545-5252

*Visa & Major Credit Cards*
*Open Daily for Dinner • Lunch Mon-Fri*

*Manager/Cellar Master*
SALVADOR TORRES
*Manager*
PATRICIA DAVIS

*Chef/Proprietor*
GUY GABRIELE

## Menu Highlights

*Appetizers*
TUNA CARPACCIO WITH
ORIENTAL SALSA • SOFT
POLENTA WITH GORGONZOLA,
MUSHROOMS & ROASTED
GARLIC • GRILLED EGGPLANT,
GOAT CHEESE, SUNDRIED
TOMATOES, SWEET ONION
& CAPERS

*Entrées*
GRILLED BABY LAMB CHOPS
IN POBLANO MARINADE
• GRILLED PEPPERED TUNA
SASHIMI WITH VEAL SOY
GINGER VINAIGRETTE

SINCE 1977, GUY GABRIELE HAS PROVIDED NEIGHBORHOOD DINERS with a serious gourmet experience in a lively, elegantly casual café near the pier in Manhattan Beach. The best of California's produce, meat and dairy products are combined with skill and refinement by Chef/proprietor Gabriele and Chef Eduardo Rodriguez, whose reduction sauces and limited fat usage are an integral part of the duo's culinary philosophy. French cooking techniques bring vigor and excitement to the lighter dishes, traditional French favorites and other globally-inspired selections. ♦ Thanks to Cellarmaster Salvador Torres, Café Pierre boasts one of Los Angeles County's top ten, four-star wine lists. An extensive wine-by-the-glass program features as many as fifteen premium wines, including selections from Australia, New Zealand and Chile. A tremendous array of French, Italian and California wines is also represented. ♦ The restaurant's light interior with skylights and ceiling fans is a perfect gallery for Gabriele's collection of stunning fauvist paintings by local artists.

**AVERAGE DINNER FOR TWO $45**
DOES NOT INCLUDE WINE, TAX AND GRATUITY

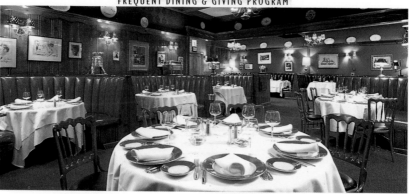

# CHASEN'S

9039 BEVERLY BOULEVARD
WEST HOLLYWOOD, CA 90048
(310) 271-2168

*Visa & Major Credit Cards*
*Dinner Tues-Sun • Lunch Tues-Fri*

*Proprietor*
MAUDE CHASEN

*Chef*
BERNARD KLERLEIN

## Menu Highlights

*Appetizers*
SMOKED SALMON
• ASSORTED SEAFOOD
PLATTER ON ICE
• FETTUCCINE WITH
MUSHROOMS &
PROSCIUTTO
*Entrées*
HOBO STEAK
• FRESH WHITEFISH
• SALMON WITH PIKE
MOUSSE • VEAL
MEDALLIONS
CALIFORNIA

A STAR FOR MORE THAN FIFTY YEARS, THE LEGENDARY CHASEN'S IS a memorial to Hollywood past and present. Opened by ex-vaudevillian Dave Chasen as a barbecue and chili joint, it evolved into a celebrity hub listing President Ronald Reagan, Liz Taylor and Frank Sinatra as regulars. ♦ "It's a cozy atmosphere," says Maude Chasen, "like your den, the place where you spend most of your time." Named "Woman of the Year" by the City of Hope charity, she still manages to spend most of her time in the restaurant, sharing its management with Ronald Clint. For more than thirty-five years, Clint has provided the comfort and attentive service patrons have come to expect from Chasen's. ♦ Chef Bernard Klerlein turns out a no-nonsense feast of signature Continental cuisine. American recipes, springing from Dave Chasen's vaudeville days, have been duplicated by Klerlein, including favorites like hobo steak. The chef has also added his own specialties to the traditional menu.

**AVERAGE DINNER FOR TWO: $80**
DOES NOT INCLUDE WINE, TAX AND GRATUITY

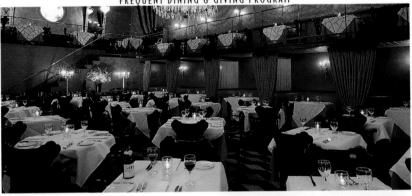

# CAFE LA BOHÈME

8400 SANTA MONICA BLVD.
AT LA CIENEGA
WEST HOLLYWOOD, CA 90069
(213) 848-2360
*Visa & Major Credit Cards*
*Open Daily • Lunch & Dinner*

*Proprietor*
KOZO HASEGAWA

*Chef*
KOICHIRO KIKUCHI
*General Manager*
TOM CARDENAS

## Menu Highlights
❦

*Appetizers*
SEARED TUNA TATAKI STYLE,
TOSA SOY SAUCE & WASABI
MAYONNAISE • PROSCIUTTO
WRAPPED MOZZARELLA GRILLED
EGGPLANT & BELL PEPPER

*Entrées*
GRILLED CHICKEN BREAST,
MASHED POTATOES & MIXED
VEGETABLES, JALAPEÑO &
CILANTRO SAUCE
• GRILLED HALIBUT &
ROCK SHRIMP WITH TOFU,
EGGPLANT & ORIENTAL SALAD,
LOBSTER & BLACK BEAN SAUCES

CAFE LA BOHÈME IS DRAMATIC IN GRAND OPERA STYLE. THE year-old restaurant's architectural details are reminiscent of a Renaissance palace or an Italian villa, with harlequin checkered walls, Promethean fireplace and appealing fountain set in a spacious room with a soaring ceiling. ♦ Having made his mark at Kyoto Miyako in Japan, Chef Koichiro Kikuchi now has a chance to experiment further without inhibition. Eating here is like sampling tastes from around the world. Italy, France and Asia contribute to the menu's extraordinary panoply of dishes, from Muscovy duck with zucchini and red cabbage to salmon served on a tortilla salad with polenta. Koichiro's goal is to "show respect for healthy, eclectic dishes beautifully presented in a dramatic setting." At Cafe La Bohème, that goal is fully realized.

**AVERAGE DINNER FOR TWO: $55**
DOES NOT INCLUDE WINE, TAX AND GRATUITY

# BREITLING
## 1884

INSTRUMENTS FOR PROFESSIONALS

At last,
perfection in a vodka.
Tanqueray Sterling.

**CALIFORNIA**
FREQUENT DINING & GIVING PROGRAM

# CAMPANILE

624 SOUTH LA BREA AVENUE
LOS ANGELES, CA 90036
(213) 938-1447

*Visa & Major Credit Cards*
*Dinner Mon-Sat • Lunch Mon-Fri • Breakfast Daily*

*Managing Partner*
MANFRED KRANKL

*Chef/Proprietors*
MARK PEEL
NANCY SILVERTON

## Menu Highlights

❦❦❦

*Appetizers*
GRILLED QUAIL WITH
GRAIN SALAD & CURLY
POTATOES • SWEET CORN
RISOTTO WITH GRILLED
SANTA BARBARA SPOT PRAWNS

*Entrées*
CRISP FLATTENED CHICKEN
WITH PARSLEY GARLIC SALAD
• CEDAR-SMOKED SALMON
WITH ARTICHOKES & WILD
MUSHROOMS • GRILLED
SWEETBREADS WITH TORN PASTA,
CHANTERELLES & TRUFFLE OIL

ONCE A STUDIO FOR CHARLIE CHAPLIN, CAMPANILE IS A 1920s three-story Moorish/Mediterranean structure with Gothic arches and a bell tower, or campanile. Guests enter through an impressive portico to an open courtyard with a tile fountain and a rainbow of flowers — a wonderful place to linger for cocktails. At street level, diners relax in an atrium set beneath a thirty-foot open skylight, while upstairs are two romantic balconies. ♦ Mark Peel and wife Nancy Silverton met while plying their talents at Michael's, then moved to Spago where Silverton was pastry chef. Her superb breads are in demand by many of L.A.'s fine restaurants and are available to the public through an adjacent bakery; her pastries and desserts can be savored in Campanile's espresso bar. ♦ Peel's eclectic California/European menu is light and unpretentious, yet full of adventure. A simple green salad embellished with sliced raw artichoke hearts and chunks of homemade toasted walnut bread is the kind of creation that brings Campanile rave reviews. So is the sourdough chocolate cake with "iced cream."

**AVERAGE DINNER FOR TWO: $70**
DOES NOT INCLUDE WINE, TAX AND GRATUITY

# CHEZ MELANGE

1716 PACIFIC COAST HIGHWAY
REDONDO BEACH, CA 90277
(310) 540-1222

*Visa & Major Credit Cards*
*Open Daily • Breakfast, Lunch & Dinner*
*Sat & Sun Brunch*

*Proprietor*
MICHAEL FRANKS
*Chef/Proprietor*
ROBERT BELL

*Chef/Proprietor*
WILLIAM DONNELLY
*Executive Chef*
MICHAEL S. SHAFER

## Menu Highlights

*Appetizers*
TURKEY JALAPEÑO SAUSAGE
WITH ROASTED TOMATO SALSA,
BLUE CORN CHIPS
• FRIED CALAMARI
• CARIBBEAN CRABCAKES
• PACIFIC RIM TOSTADAS

*Entrées*
SPICY MEATLOAF
WITH RED WINE SAUCE
• "PYRAMID" HEART
HEALTHY SPECIALS
• JERK CHICKEN
• NEW ENGLAND PORK LOIN

AS ITS NAME IMPLIES, CHEZ MELANGE IS A MIXTURE OF EVERYTHING under the sun. "We make each day a celebration," says owner Michael Franks, "in order to keep the feeling of newness, freshness, excitement and electricity." ♦ The menu represents Chef Robert Bell's intrepid forays into international fare. His daily offerings are so numerous that getting around to the featured cuisines could take several visits. That's just what Bell and Franks intended. ♦ When the two met in England, they realized they shared a common goal: to open a restaurant that would deliver both diversity and consistent quality. All breads, desserts, sausages and pasta are made on the premises. The decor ranges from gentle peach shades to high-tech white on white. In keeping with the dynamic owners' goal, Chez Melange is more an experience than an establishment. ♦ Their newest venture, Depot, with talented Chef Michael Shafer in the kitchen, is another success story in the making.

**AVERAGE DINNER FOR TWO: $45**
DOES NOT INCLUDE WINE, TAX AND GRATUITY

**CALIFORNIA/CHINESE**
FREQUENT DINING & GIVING PROGRAM

# CHINOIS ON MAIN

2709 MAIN STREET
SANTA MONICA, CA 90405
(310) 392-9025

*This restaurant prefers Visa*
*Open Daily for Dinner • Lunch Wed-Fri*

*Manager*
BELLA LANTSMAN

*Chef*
MAKOTO TANAKA

## Menu Highlights
▼▼▼

*Appetizers*
FRESH GOOSE LIVER
WITH MARINATED, GRILLED
PINEAPPLES • WARM SWEET
CURRIED OYSTERS WITH
CUCUMBER SAUCE & SALMON
PEARLS • SZECHUAN PANCAKES
WITH STIR-FRIED DUCK,
MUSHROOMS & CILANTRO

*Entrées*
WHOLE SIZZLING CATFISH
STUFFED WITH GINGER
• GRILLED MONGOLIAN
LAMB CHOPS WITH
CILANTRO VINAIGRETTE &
WOK-FRIED VEGETABLES

WHEN WOLFGANG PUCK OPENED SPAGO IN 1981 AND ELEVATED pizza to haute California cuisine, he attained the stature of Southern California's most influential chef. Two years later, Puck launched Chinois on Main to celebrate the official marriage of Eastern and Western cuisines. Today, the union of Chinese ingredients and French techniques no longer startles, and Chinois maintains the romance with unsurpassed success. ♦ Although Puck sets the guidelines, Chef Makoto Tanaka has the freedom to create recipes, fine tune the menu and improvise daily specials. The special Chinois style includes surprisingly good desserts (including three kinds of crème brulée). ♦ The striking decor was created by Puck's interior designer wife, Barbara Lazaroff. Chinois is always packed, and no wonder. It's one of a kind.

**AVERAGE DINNER FOR TWO: $100**
DOES NOT INCLUDE WINE, TAX AND GRATUITY

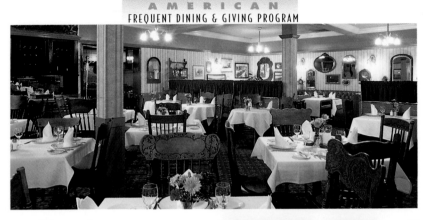

AMERICAN
FREQUENT DINING & GIVING PROGRAM

# THE CHRONICLE

897 GRANITE DRIVE
PASADENA, CA 91101
(818) 792-1179

*Visa & Major Credit Cards*
*Open Daily for Dinner • Lunch Mon-Sat*

| | |
|---|---|
| *Managing Partner* | *Chef* |
| ROGER RENICK | DOMENICK MEDINA |

## Menu Highlights

*Appetizers*

THIN CRISP POTATOES, ONIONS & PARSLEY WITH SMOKED SALMON, CAVIAR & SOUR CREAM

*Entrées*

FRESH SALMON SAUTÉED WITH BLACK PEPPER WITH SPINACH & PEARL ONIONS WITH ROASTED GARLIC CREAM SAUCE

• ROASTED SADDLE OF LAMB FOR TWO WITH ROSEMARY & BOUQUET OF VEGETABLES

ON A TINY STREET IN DOWNTOWN PASADENA IS THE CHRONICLE, a local landmark for more than twenty years. The restaurant pays tribute to turn-of-the-century San Francisco, with brass lamps, leaded glass and embossed tin ceilings. Its walls and cozy, semiprivate nooks are hung with period photographs and era newspaper clippings. ♦ The focal point of this nostalgic restaurant is a large four-sided bar, nearly always hidden behind a large gathering of loyal patrons. The Chronicle's "regulars" are drawn both to its friendly atmosphere and the classic contemporary American fare created by its chef of twenty years, Domenick Medina, whose presence is an important part of The Chronicle experience. ♦ Medina's hearty cuisine is rounded out by fresh seafood specialties and complemented by an incredible wine list. Winner of *The Wine Spectator's* Grand Award for eleven consecutive years, the 95-page categorized list is, as owner Lud Renick proudly states, "The best of the best."

**AVERAGE DINNER FOR TWO: $55**
DOES NOT INCLUDE WINE, TAX AND GRATUITY

40

# CICADA

8478 MELROSE AVENUE
AT CLINTON
WEST HOLLYWOOD, CA 90069
(213) 655-5559
*Visa & Major Credit Cards*
*Lunch Mon-Fri • Dinner Mon-Sat*

*Proprietor*
STEPHANIE HAYMES

*Chef/Proprietor*
JEAN-FRANÇOIS
METEIGNER

## Menu Highlights

*Appetizers*
NORWEGIAN SMOKED SALMON
• HEARTS OF ROMAINE &
BELGIAN ENDIVE WITH
ROQUEFORT & WHITE
TRUFFLE OIL DRESSING

*Entrées*
MUSCOVY DUCK
COOKED TWO WAYS WITH
HONEY-ORANGE SAUCE
• ROASTED RACK OF LAMB FOR
TWO SERVED WITH MUSTARD &
BLACK OLIVE SAUCE, ROASTED
POTATOES • RISOTTO WITH
GRILLED SCALLOPS & VANILLA
LOBSTER BEAN SAUCE

IT IS SAID THAT IN FRANCE A CICADA IS A SYMBOL FOR GOOD luck. Stephanie Haymes and Chef Jean-François Meteigner, of Le Dôme and L'Orangerie fame respectively, have teamed up with rock legend Bernie Taupin to produce one of the most charming restaurants on Melrose Avenue. Calling it Cicada is their way of keeping in favor with the gods. ♦ With its soothing decor and subtle stencil motif, the main room hosts a bevy of celebrities who come in search of Meteigner's succulent veal chops and mouth-watering fresh seafood. From Maryland crabcakes to lobster and rock shrimp sausage in lime sauce, the chef's dishes bring delicate flavors and elegance to this new venue. The semi-private back room is the restaurant's hot spot, featuring a graceful bar and complete catering service. ♦ Spawned at two undeniable Los Angeles institutions, the combined talent at Cicada represents a new generation of restaurateurs. Yes, their enviable reservation list is a sign of good fortune — but it's also the result of a lot of hard work and experience.

**AVERAGE DINNER FOR TWO: $65**
DOES NOT INCLUDE WINE, TAX AND GRATUITY

# CITRUS

6703 MELROSE AVENUE
LOS ANGELES, CA 90038
(213) 857-0034

*Visa & Major Credit Cards
Lunch Mon-Fri • Dinner Mon-Sat*

*General Manager*
ROBERT FAUVE

*Chef/Proprietor*
MICHEL RICHARD

## Menu Highlights

*Appetizers*
SHIITAKE MUSHROOM
& GARLIC TART
• SMOKED SALMON
TERRINE • SNAILS
IN A BASKET

*Entrées*
GRILLED SWORDFISH
MINESTRONE
• SCALLOP PIE • VEAL
WITH MASHED POTATOES
& HORSERADISH
SAUCE • MEDALLIONS
OF PEPPERED TUNA
SERVED RARE WITH
SAUCE POIVRADE

IN THIS CITY OF GLITZ, GLAMOUR AND RESTAURANTS ALL VYING for attention, Citrus is a show-stopper, a definite must for devotees of the California bistro scene. Owned by master patissier Michel Richard, Citrus has all the right ingredients for success, not the least of which is Richard's status as a brilliant chef. ♦ A lively restaurant, Citrus provides a bright, sun-filled environment for L.A.'s gourmets and trendsetters to enjoy Richard's contemporary French fare. The chic eatery is white-washed from floor to ceiling and has a large, lively sundeck tented with white canvas umbrellas. ♦ In his ultramodern open kitchen, Richard creates stylish cuisine that mirrors the mood of his restaurant perfectly: elegant, imaginative and unpretentious. He constantly strives to perfect his menu, paying close attention to both media reviews and feedback from his fashionable clientele. His disciplined technique leaves no room for bizarre culinary combinations; it is superb cuisine, strikingly presented.

**AVERAGE DINNER FOR TWO: $85**
DOES NOT INCLUDE WINE, TAX AND GRATUITY

# ChristianDior

# To improve this meal, just add water.

The perfect accompaniment to an exquisite meal is an equally exquisite beverage. Quite naturally, we recommend Evian, from the French Alps.

Evian's purity makes it clear, light, and refreshing. Which means it will make a delightful complement to any meal at any time. And it has the wonderful ability to cleanse the palate between courses, and wines.

Besides, Evian is natural spring water without bubbles. So you won't feel filled up when you drink it.

That's why, if good food graces your table, so should Evian.

**E V I A N.  T H E  B A L A N C E.™**

# DRAGO

2628 WILSHIRE BLVD.
26TH STREET
SANTA MONICA, CA 90403
(310) 828-1585

*Visa & Major Credit Cards*
*Open Daily for Dinner • Lunch Mon-Fri*

*Managers*
ISSAC RIVERA
CALOGERO DRAGO

*Proprietor/Chef*
CELESTINO DRAGO

## Menu Highlights

*Appetizers*

SOUP MADE WITH BORLOTTI
BEANS & FARRO WHEAT
• SANTA BARBARA SHRIMPS
WRAPPED WITH PROSCIUTTO
IN A BED OF GREEN LENTILS
• SMOKED SWORDFISH CARPAC-
CIO WITH CUCUMBER SALAD

*Entrées*

PAPPARDELLE WITH
PHEASANT SAUCE & MORELS
• SWEET POTATO GNOCCHI WITH
LOBSTER & ARUGULA • ROASTED
RABBIT WITH BELL PEPPERS &
BLACK OLIVES • VENISON IN FIG
SAUCE WITH POLENTA

IF YOU'RE IN THE MOOD FOR A MEAL PREPARED BY CELEBRATED Chef Celestino Drago, look no further than his new restaurant. No longer involved with Celestino's, Drago has designed his own showcase for food that inevitably earns raves no matter where he cooks it. An easy dining room features clean, elegant lines, blonde wood accents and an airy glass façade. ♦ Born in Sicily, the chef came of age in the kitchens of Pisa before arriving in Los Angeles to develop menus for Orlando Orsini's and Chianti Cucina. Although his subsequent success at Celestino brought him renown, his current solo venture gives him the most satisfaction. "This is the restaurant I've always wanted," says Drago, "my menu has a little of everything from all over Italy." The Sicilian dishes are the kind you might find strolling the beaches below Mt. Etna: spaghetti with sardines and wild fennel, or cured, dried tuna roe nicknamed "Sicilian Caviar." Drago's latest menu features *Farro*, a wheat so precious, it was once used as currency in ancient Rome.

**AVERAGE DINNER FOR TWO: $60**
DOES NOT INCLUDE WINE, TAX AND GRATUITY

# DC-3

2800 DONALD DOUGLAS LOOP NORTH
SANTA MONICA, CA 90405
(310) 399-2323
*Visa & Major Credit Cards*
*Dinner Mon–Sat • Lunch Mon–Fri • Sunday Brunch*

*Proprietor*
DAVID PRICE

*Chef*
BILL HUFFERD

## Menu Highlights

*Appetizers*
LENTIL SOUP WITH ITALIAN SAUSAGE • STEAK CARPACCIO WITH ARUGULA LEAVES, PARMESAN & OLIVE OIL • SMOKED SALMON POTATO PANCAKE

*Entrées*
CHARRED RACK OF LAMB WITH POLENTA & PANCETTA • PENNE WITH TOMATO, BASIL & GARLIC • GRILLED JUMBO SHRIMP WITH LEMON & THYME, SERVED WITH SPINACH TART

ATTRACTED BY DC-3's CREATIVE AMERICAN CUISINE AND STRIKING architecture, Hollywood and Westside crowds fill the airy dining room with its exciting view of planes taking off and landing on the runway of Santa Monica Airport. Three-dimensional modern art pieces and vintage motorcycles complement the restaurant's aeronautical motif. ♦ Executive Chef William Hufferd fuses grilled American specialties with classical technique, accented with a range of ethnic touches from France, Italy and Asia. Exciting, flexible and enduring, it invites experimentation. Born and raised in Los Angeles, Chef Hufferd stays true to his California roots choosing only fresh, local ingredients to create his simple, elegant menu. Whether it's a crisp, full-flavored Caesar salad or swordfish grilled over a pungent wood fire and served with a lemon basil sauce, his dishes delight the senses. ♦ Outdoor dining overlooking the Pacific and the adjacent Museum of Flying, scene of many film industry galas, are additional draws.

**AVERAGE DINNER FOR TWO: $55**
DOES NOT INCLUDE WINE, TAX AND GRATUITY

46

## CONTINENTAL
### FREQUENT DINING & GIVING PROGRAM

# DYNASTY

WESTWOOD MARQUIS HOTEL
930 HILGARD AVENUE
WESTWOOD, CA 90024
(310) 208-8765
*Visa & Major Credit Cards*
*Dinner Only • Mon–Sat*

*Maître d'*
GEORGE SKORKA

*Executive Chef*
SIGI SCHAFNER

## Menu Highlights

*Appetizers*
CRISP POTATO PANCAKE
WITH HOUSE-SMOKED SALMON
• CHARRED SHRIMP WITH
ASPARAGUS, ARTICHOKE &
BALSAMIC VINAIGRETTE

*Entrées*
GRILLED STRIPED BASS WITH
JAPANESE EGGPLANT, RAGOUT
WITH HERBS & MINT • SEAFOOD
MIXED GRILL WITH LOBSTER,
HALIBUT, SCALLOPS & MUSSELS
• PEKING-STYLE DUCK WITH
FRIED NOODLES & PLUM SAUCE

AUSTRIAN-BORN CHEF SIGI SCHAFNER AND DINNER CHEF REZA Motamednia have turned the elegant top floor dining room of the celebrity studded Westwood Marquis Hotel into a delightful destination at the edge of UCLA. Schafner's love for hearty home cooking is apparent at first glance of the menu and particularly expressed with his scallops and lentils, a dish he calls "fancy, home cooking." All sauces are made on the premises and specialties of the day might be a seared filet of veal with black bean cake and tomatillo sauce, or crispy Ahi tuna with spicy Bannan salsa and curried couscous. ◆ The main dining area is an attractive combination of fine art and burnished woods, and original drawings by Erté adorn Dynasty's semi-private room. Semi-circular boothes add cozy appeal. Count on immaculate service at all times thanks to charming Maître d' George Skorka.

### AVERAGE DINNER FOR TWO: $60
DOES NOT INCLUDE WINE, TAX AND GRATUITY

# EMPORIO ARMANI EXPRESS

9533 BRIGHTON WAY
AT RODEO DRIVE
BEVERLY HILLS, CA 90210
(310) 271-9940
*Visa & Major Credit Cards*
*Open Daily • Lunch & Dinner*

*General Manager*
ROBERTO ROSSI

*Chef*
ANTONIO MATTINA

## Menu Highlights

*Appetizers*
DEEP-FRIED ZUCCHINI
WITH PROSCIUTTO & PORCINI
IN TOMATO SAUCE • WARMED
GARLIC, ANCHOVIES & OLIVE
OIL DIP SERVED WITH RAW
VEGETABLES & MEAT

*Entrées*
SAUTÉED VENISON
TENDERLOIN WITH COGNAC &
PORCINI • SALMON WRAPPED &
BAKED IN PARCHMENT PAPER
WITH FRESH ORANGE SLICES &
BABY CHIVES • RACK OF LAMB
TOPPED WITH ARTICHOKE
HEARTS & LAMB SAUCE

NESTLED INCONSPICUOUSLY ABOVE THE BEVERLY HILLS ARMANI clothing store, Emporio Armani Express is a tasteful, elegant and understated restaurant befitting the Armani name. Managed with precision by Roberto Rossi, formerly of Prego, the small restaurant offers a splendid view of the Beverly Hills shopping district below. ♦ Sicilian by birth and Milanese by training, Chef Antonio Mattina has created a menu that explores the best of authentic Italian cuisine. Specials include branzino, broiled and served whole then deboned at the table. Pay attention to the *risotto al martini* served with a shot of white vermouth guaranteed to stimulate the palate. ♦ Desserts such as zuccottino, baby pumpkin-shaped genoise filled with chocolate mascarpone, or the addictive "Aida," with crispy caramelized walnuts baked on a warm dark chocolate cake, deserve more than a taste.

**AVERAGE DINNER FOR TWO: $60**
DOES NOT INCLUDE WINE, TAX AND GRATUITY

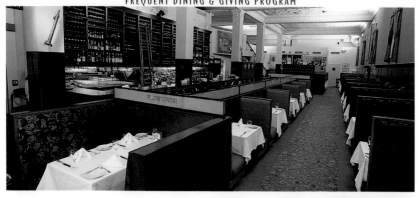

# ENGINE CO. NO. 28

644 SOUTH FIGUEROA STREET
LOS ANGELES, CA 90017
(213) 624-6996

*Visa & Major Credit Cards*
*Dinner Mon-Sat • Lunch Mon-Fri*

| General Manager | Chef |
|:---:|:---:|
| ED KASKY | CHRIS FERRELL |

## Menu Highlights

*Appetizers*
CAESAR SALAD
• SPICY FRIES
• FRENCH FRIED ONIONS
• FIREHOUSE OYSTERS
• VEGETABLE ANTIPASTO

*Entrées*
WHISKEY-FENNEL SAUSAGES
• DRY-AGED NEW YORK STEAK
• MEATLOAF WITH
MASHED POTATOES
• MARYLAND CRABCAKES
• GRILLED SWORDFISH

ENGINE CO. NO. 28, A FAVORITE GATHERING SPOT DOWNTOWN, IS a 1912 firehouse lovingly restored with attention to detail by owners Linda Griego, Peter Mullin and Jerry Magnin. The three worked closely together to preserve the best memorabilia and turned the old engine room into a mahogany clubhouse full of warmth and lively elegance. ♦ Lunchers suspend power politics at a friendly bar offering many fine beers, bourbons and single-malt scotches, as well as an impressive wine selection, before sampling the wide-ranging American grill specialties. After dinner, downtowners cozy up to apple pie, chocolate pudding and other old-fashioned desserts. ♦ "I wanted to create a place where customers could eat every day no matter what their mood," says General Manager Ed Kasky. "I like restaurants that you can go back to again and again, ordering pasta one night, steak the next and seafood another time—eventually trying everything on the menu."

**AVERAGE DINNER FOR TWO: $50**
DOES NOT INCLUDE WINE, TAX AND GRATUITY

49

**CALIFORNIA/FRENCH**
FREQUENT DINING & GIVING PROGRAM

# FOUR OAKS

2181 NORTH BEVERLY GLEN
LOS ANGELES, CA 90077
(310) 470-2265

*Visa & MasterCard Only*
*Dinner Mon–Sun • Lunch Tues–Sat • Sunday Brunch*

| *Maître d'* | *Chef/Proprietor* |
| MICHEL PERETZ | PETER ROELANT |

## Menu Highlights

*Appetizers*
CORN CHOWDER WITH ROASTED
BELL PEPPER & CILANTRO
• SASHIMI TUNA CARPACCIO
WITH HORSERADISH &
MUSTARD DRESSING,
JAPANESE CUCUMBER SALAD

*Entrées*
CRUSHED PEPPER VENISON FILET
WITH LIME-BRANDY-WALNUT
SAUCE & HUNTER'S GARNISHES
• HONEY-NUT CRUSTED
OVEN-ROASTED LAMB, BELL
PEPPER FLAN & GARLIC WITH
BACON HARICOTS VERT

IF ESCAPING TO A RUSTIC RETREAT IN A CENTURY-OLD HOUSE dwarfed by fragrant eucalyptus and sycamore trees is in order, try the Four Oaks. Tucked away in a small Bel Air canyon just a quick jaunt from Sunset Boulevard, this restaurant is as charming as it is excellent. ♦ Contemporary French food bursting with fresh, lively combinations, and an exquisitely compiled wine list are only part of the lure of Four Oaks. Chef Peter Roelant, from the famed Girardet in Switzerland and L'Orangerie in Los Angeles, commands his menu as a poet would a pen, presenting with flair signature dishes such as foie gras sautéed with plums and raspberry vinegar. ♦ Maître d' Yann Peron, a native of France, is on hand day and night to greet guests and synchronize the restaurant's unassuming, superior service.

**AVERAGE DINNER FOR TWO: $80**
DOES NOT INCLUDE WINE, TAX AND GRATUITY

## THE TANK WATCH.

### THE ART OF BEING UNIQUE.

# Cartier

## JOAILLIERS SINCE 1847

·EST· ·1822·

**FONSECA GUIMARAENS**

·VINHOS S.A·

·OPORTO·PORTUGAL·

# FONSECA
# BIN Nº 27

*Fine Reserve*

# PORT

BOTTLED IN OPORTO     PRODUCT OF PORTUGAL

# GRANITA

23725 WEST MALIBU ROAD
MALIBU COLONY PLAZA
MALIBU, CA 90265
(310) 456-0488

*This restaurant prefers Visa*
*Dinner Daily • Lunch Wed-Fri • Sat & Sun Brunch*

*Proprietor* — *Chef*
BARBARA LAZAROFF — KEVIN RIPLEY

## Menu Highlights

*Appetizers*
RED & YELLOW GAZPACHO
WITH CHILLED MARINATED
PRAWNS • GRAVLAX WITH NEW
POTATOES & SPICY MSUTARD
SAUCE • GRILLED DUCK SAUSAGE
WITH GRANNY SMITH APPLES
& SPICY GREENS

*Entrées*
POTATO GALETTE WITH
SCRAMBLED EGG & GRAVLAX
• GRILLED PRAWNS WITH
ANGELHAIR PASTA & TOMATO,
BASIL FONDUE • GRILLED
CHICKEN BREAST WITH
ARUGULA & WATERCRESS WITH
MANGO VINAIGRETTE

FIRST IT WAS SPAGO, THEN CHINOIS ON MAIN AND A SMASH HIT called Postrio. Now it's Granita. Barbara Lazaroff and Wolfgang Puck's newest Los Angeles venture, which means a fruity, frozen concoction enjoyed in warm climates, embodies the look, feel and palate of the world's most romantic temperate zone, the Mediterranean. Near the ocean and a picturesque garden redolent with the scent of fresh herbs, Granita manifests a languid mood. ♦ The restaurant's actual location: Malibu. Lazaroff's trademark open kitchen, outdoor dining area and dramatic landscaping visually set the 160-seat restaurant apart. Breezy seaside pastels, skylights, undulating curves and glazed tiles create what she calls "an abstract interpretation of the water, its changing elements of light and underwater movement." ♦ Puck's seasonal menu emphasizes fresh seafood dishes with the flavors of Provence, Tuscany and Southern Italy. As always, he has assembled a top-notch staff with impeccable credentials. The restaurant's wine list, too, emphasizes Mediterranean regions.

**AVERAGE DINNER FOR TWO: $65**
DOES NOT INCLUDE WINE, TAX AND GRATUITY

ITALIAN
FREQUENT DINING & GIVING PROGRAM

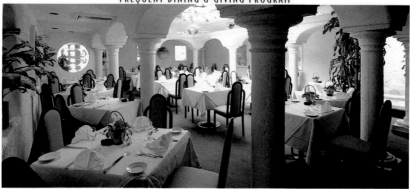

# FRESCO RISTORANTE

514 SOUTH BRAND BOULEVARD
GLENDALE, CA 91204
(818) 247-5541

*Visa & Major Credit Cards*
*Dinner Mon–Sat • Lunch Mon–Fri*

*Maître d'*
KEVIN BROWN

*Chef/Proprietor*
ANTONIO ORLANDO

## Menu Highlights

*Appetizers*
CRESPELLE STUFFED WITH DUCK
IN A PORT & PORCINI SAUCE
• ZUCCHINI STUFFED WITH
MASCARPONE CHEESE
• WARM VEAL LIVER WITH
SEASONAL BERRIES

*Entrées*
TAGLIOLINI WITH WHITE
TRUFFLES • MEDALLION OF
VENISON WITH JUNIPER BERRY
SAUCE • RISOTTO WITH PORCINI
& RADICCHIO

A SLICE OF THE SUNNY SKY-LIT MEDITERRANEAN BY DAY, AND A warm, intimate oasis by night, the renowned Fresco is back. With his uncompromising passion for Italian cuisine, the restaurant's original chef, Antonio Orlando, is again in the kitchen cooking up his acclaimed risotto, pasta and seafood dishes. He's added wild game creations and seasonal delicacies, such as white or black truffles, to a menu that smacks of his unique and light approach to savory, yet health-conscious, fine dining. ♦ An extensive selection of grappas, aperitifs and cognacs served at the piano bar, open until the wee hours, gives the new Fresco fresh excitement. Says Maitre d' Kevin Brown, "We are here to please our customers with fine food and indulgent service, offering them a memorable evening that makes them want to come back."

**AVERAGE DINNER FOR TWO: $50**
DOES NOT INCLUDE WINE, TAX AND GRATUITY

# THE GRILL
ON THE ALLEY

9560 DAYTON WAY
BEVERLY HILLS, CA 90210
(310) 276-0615

*Visa & Major Credit Cards*
*Closed Sunday • Lunch & Dinner*

| *Proprietors* | *Chef* |
| BOB SPIVAK | TONY HIPP |
| ALLAN LUDWIG | |

## Menu Highlights
(▼▼)

*Appetizers*

SHRIMP COCKTAIL • BAKED
CLAMS • GRAVLAX • STEAK
TARTARE • SAUTÉED BAY
SCALLOPS • CARPACCIO

*Entrées*

NEW YORK STEAK, CHARCOAL-
BROILED • BROILED HALF-
CHICKEN • PAN-FRIED
WHITEFISH • CALF'S LIVER
WITH BACON & ONIONS
• POT ROAST & POTATO
PANCAKES • BRAISED
SHORT-RIBS • CHARCOAL-
BROILED SWORDFISH

WHAT'S AN OLD-TIME AMERICAN RESTAURANT LIKE THE GRILL doing in fashion-conscious Beverly Hills? That's what the skeptics asked when The Grill opened. They said it was out of place, too simple of decor and menu to attract a following. Luckily for everyone, they were wrong, and the restaurant has been packed with a regular clientele — including a huge following of celebrities — ever since. ♦ Bob Spivak, a restaurant veteran who trained for twelve years with his father, understood the concept and how to create it: from the classic dining room with its handsome mahogany bar, wooden booths and black-and-white floor, to the all-American menu with its huge portions, perfectly grilled steaks and hearty side dishes prepared in a kitchen open to view. ♦ "We wanted a very honest, straightforward restaurant," says Spivak. They have succeeded with The Grill.

**AVERAGE DINNER FOR TWO: $70**
DOES NOT INCLUDE WINE, TAX AND GRATUITY

# I CUGINI

1501 OCEAN AVENUE
SANTA MONICA, CA 90401
(310) 451-4595

*Visa & Major Credit Cards*
*Open Daily • Lunch & Dinner*

General Manager
CARLA UGOLINI

Chef
JOE VENEZIA

## Menu Highlights

*Appetizers*
MIXED VEGETABLE ANTIPASTI
• PASTA WITH SHRIMPS,
MUSSELS, CLAMS, SCALLOPS &
SQUID • FRIED CALAMARI

*Entrées*
GRILLED SALMON
WITH FRIED SPINACH, RED
ONIONS & PANCETTA
• MARINATED QUAIL WITH PINK
PEPPERCORNS & POLENTA
• OSSO BUCO TRIESTINA
WITH PORCINI, SWEET PEAS &
MASHED POTATOES

WITH PERHAPS THE BEST VIEW ON THE WEST SIDE OF LOS Angeles, I Cugini serves some of the best Italian food anywhere. The ocean is a feast for the eyes while the kitchen, equipped for multi-course meals or a light bite, tantalizes all the senses with unforgettable plates of pleasure. ♦ An open-air kitchen provides entertainment while guests wait in mouth-watering anticipation. Joe Venezia, former chef at the Hotel Bel Air, features hearty, flavorful and sophisticated Northern Italian specialties and more than twenty different pasta dishes daily. A selection of breads is freshly baked and served with a delicious olive purée. ♦ Celebrities, out-of-towners and locals match wits with outgoing Manager Carla Ugolini as they settle in for a lively meal. If you're so inclined and the timing is right, ask to dine *al fresco* while watching the orange sun slip into the Pacific.

**AVERAGE DINNER FOR TWO: $40**
DOES NOT INCLUDE WINE, TAX AND GRATUITY

# LA CHAUMIÈRE

CENTURY PLAZA HOTEL & TOWER
2055 AVENUE OF THE STARS
LOS ANGELES, CA 90067
(310) 551-3360

*Visa & Major Credit Cards*
*Dinner Daily • Lunch Mon–Fri*

| *Manager* | *Chef* |
|---|---|
| IRAJ "ROGER" AKHAVAN | TADASHI KATOH |

## Menu Highlights
❧

*Appetizers*
SCOTTISH SMOKED SALMON, HORSERADISH & CAPER CREAM
• CHAMPAGNE RISOTTO & WILD FOREST MUSHROOMS
• CREAM OF SPINACH & HERBS

*Entrées*
PAN-FRIED WHITE FISH, SNOW PEAS & BELGIUM ENDIVE, MERLOT & TARRAGON BUTTER SAUCE • POACHED BREAST OF CHICKEN WITH VEGETABLES IN CLEAR BROTH • BROILED SWORDFISH ON RATATOUILLE, CHIVE BUTTER SAUCE

THERE'S A CHARMING REFUGE FROM THE GLITZ AND BUSTLE OF Century City's theatre and cinema complex at the landmark Century Plaza Hotel. La Chaumière, or country retreat, is intimate and gracious, rare attributes for a hotel restaurant. A separate entrance and private elevator with trompe-l'oeil walls and ceiling lead to a bar that is ideal for fireside cocktails before a show, or after-dinner cordials. ♦ Five mural-sized, eighteenth century pastoral paintings lend a timeless air to the main dining room paneled in alder wood. A beautiful hand-knotted floral rug and burled elm chairs create a warm comfortable atmosphere. For sweeping vistas while dining, La Chaumière's curving wintergarden overlooks terraced hills, orange-tiled rooftops and Santa Monica Bay beyond. A richly appointed private room is separated from the main room by beveled glass doors. ♦ Executive Chef Tadashi Katoh's Provençal classics emphasize the quality and flavor of raw ingredients, and his elegant presentation underscores La Chaumière's inherent simplicity and grace.

**AVERAGE DINNER FOR TWO: $80**
DOES NOT INCLUDE WINE, TAX & GRATUITY

**ITALIAN**
FREQUENT DINING & GIVING PROGRAM

# LA LUNA RISTORANTE

113 NORTH LARCHMONT BLVD.
LOS ANGELES, CA 90004
(213) 962-2130

*Visa & Major Credit Cards*
*Mon–Sat • Lunch & Dinner*
*• Sunday Dinner Only*

*Proprietors*
FRANCESCO PRUNALI
THERESA KIM
ANTONIO VISCITO

*Chef /Proprietor*
ROBERTINO
GIOVANNELLI

## Menu Highlights

*Appetizers*
MUSHROOMS & GOAT CHEESE
WRAPPED IN PUFF PASTRY
WITH WARM CREAMY
MUSHROOM SAUCE
• TUNA CARPACCIO WITH
MIXED BABY GREENS

*Entrées*
HOUSEMADE PASTA WITH
SHRIMP & ARTICHOKES
• VEAL CHOP WRAPPED
IN RADICCHIO LEAF
IN WHITE WINE SAUCE
• PIZZA WITH MOZZARELLA,
TOMATOES, MUSHROOMS &
DUCK SAUSAGE

LA LUNA COMBINES MODERN ARCHITECTURAL STYLING WITH SIMPLE, yet terrific Northern California cuisine. Located at the south end of the Larchmont District, the restaurant is resplendent with skylights, hand-made ceramic tiles and fountains. A metal counter topped with granite and numerous fresco paintings of flowers and angels grace the walls, and brick columns complement the stained wood ceilings and metal fixtures. The overall effect is very rustic with contemporary accents. ♦ Chef/Pro-prietor Robertino Giovannelli continues this dance of traditional and new in the restaurant's open kitchen. "We want customers to understand pure Italian food as it was meant to be served, and we prepare light, fresh dishes right before their eyes," says Giovannelli. "Everything is made at the moment; nothing is done in advance." ♦ The place is bustling with a casual and sophisticated clientele who find La Luna absolutely comfort-able thanks to the sense of neighborhood that permeates. Friendly and polished, proprietor Francesco Prunali is a constant and warm presence with personal greetings for everyone who enters his restaurant.

**AVERAGE DINNER FOR TWO: $45**
DOES NOT INCLUDE WINE, TAX AND GRATUITY

# LALIQUE

Seau à Champagne Ganymede

The only Lalique boutique in the United States.
We gladly ship nationwide.

## LALIQUE BOUTIQUE
680 Madison Avenue • New York, N.Y. 10021
1-800-214-2738

*In FRANCE, there is a special word for Aperitif.*

LILLET,
*The Spirit of Bordeaux*

# LA RIVE GAUCHE

320 TEJON PLACE
PALOS VERDES ESTATES, CA 90274
(213) 378-0267
*Visa & Major Credit Cards*
*Open Daily for Dinner • Lunch Tues-Sun*

*Proprietors*
ANNA MARTIN
ANDRÉ MARTIN

*Maître d*
AL CASTANEDA
*Chef*
DAVID LIBBY

### Menu Highlights
♣♥

*Appetizers*
WARM CORNBREAD BLINI
WITH CREME FRAICHE, CAVIAR &
SMOKED SALMON
• SONOMA RABBIT PATÉ

*Entrées*
VEAL CHOP WITH MOREL
COGNAC CREAM SAUCE
• BLACKENED AHI
WITH MANGO, GINGER,
CILANTRO & LIME SAUCE
• STUFFED BREAST OF
PHEASANT WITH WILD
MUSHROOMS IN COGNAC
GLAZE SAUCE

AT THE SOUTHERNMOST TIP OF THE CURVING SOUTH BAY LIES Palos Verdes, quite possibly the most beautiful stretch of mountains meeting surf in the Los Angeles area. Hidden among the green hills and sheltered estate homes is La Rive Gauche. ♦ Opened sixteen years ago by partners André Martin, La Rive Gauche captures the French country style. A long dining room lined with windows looks out over quaint Tejon Place, and a peaceful terrace inspires outdoor dining. At night, candlelight and delicate harp music blend to create an air of romance and tranquility. ♦ Manager Al Castaneda has a warm welcome for everyone, and his highly skilled staff is devoted to excellence. Chef David Libby favors classic French cuisine and believes that attention to details is critical to the success of his preparations. A spectacular wine list of 1,000 premier labels in all price ranges has earned La Rive Gauche *The Wine Spectator* Grand Award since 1984, ranking it as one of the nation's top ten lists.

**AVERAGE DINNER FOR TWO: $75**
DOES NOT INCLUDE WINE, TAX AND GRATUITY

# LE CHARDONNAY

8284 MELROSE AVENUE
LOS ANGELES, CA 90046
(213) 655-8880

*Visa & Major Credit Cards*
*Closed Sunday • Lunch & Dinner*

*Proprietor*
ROBERT BIGONNET

*Chef/Proprietor*
CLAUDE ALRIVY

## Menu Highlights

*Appetizers*
WARM CRISPY SWEETBREAD
SALAD WITH OYSTER
MUSHROOMS &
SNOWPEAS • RAVIOLI
WITH CALIFORNIA
PETIT GRIS SNAILS
& GARLIC SAUCE

*Entrées*
PEKING DUCK
ON THE SPIT WITH HONEY
& GINGER SAUCE • MEDALLIONS
OF VENISON SAUTÉED
WITH BLACK PEPPERCORN,
CELERY ROOT FRITTERS
& ARMAGNAC PEPPER SAUCE

THE ADDRESS MAY BE MELROSE AVENUE, BUT THE SPIRIT AND FARE are definitely Boulevard Saint-Germain. Conceived by Robert Bigonnet and Claude Alrivy as an elegant, Parisian-style bistro, Le Chardonnay has colorful old French tiles, huge arched mirrors and a visible rotisserie. ♦ A talented twosome, Alrivy and Bigonnet left the celebrated Le St. Germain to recreate Bigonnet's favorite Left Bank café. They spared no detail — from the heady, garlic-infused bouillabaisse to the expertly duplicated wood paintings adorning the dining room walls — and Le Chardonnay soon became one of the city's French hot spots. ♦ Artfully prepared with an occasional spin to the left, Le Chardonnay's menu boasts an array of traditional as well as innovative dishes. Desserts, such as a warm raspberry napoleon with raspberry coulis, are always captivating. For lovers of Chardonnay, the wine list has more than forty-five selections.

**AVERAGE DINNER FOR TWO: $70**
DOES NOT INCLUDE WINE, TAX AND GRATUITY

**CONTINENTAL**
FREQUENT DINING & GIVING PROGRAM

# L'ESCOFFIER

BEVERLY HILTON HOTEL
9876 WILSHIRE BOULEVARD
BEVERLY HILLS, CA 90210
(310) 285-1333
*Visa & Major Credit Cards*
*Dinner Tues–Sat*

*Manager*
FERNAND

*Chef*
MICHEL BLANCHET

## Menu Highlights

*Appetizers*
LANGOUSTINE ANGEL HAIR
PASTA WITH BASIL & TOMATO
• OYSTERS TARTAR WITH TWO
CAVIARS • VICHYSSOISE

*Entrées*
SAUTÉED SEABASS
ON LENTILS WITH BLACK
BUTTER VINAIGRETTE • BAKED
TOURNEDOS OF CHICKEN IN
CURRY & COCONUT SAUCE
• ROASTED RACK OF LAMB WITH
FRESH THYME CRUST

REDESIGNED IN FEBRUARY OF 1991 AND AWARDED A PRESTIGIOUS four-star rating from the California Restaurant Writers' Association, the fanciful atmosphere of L'Escoffier is now highlighted by country French touches and mirrors to maximize the restaurant's breathtaking view. Open since the hotel's debut in 1955, L'Escoffier has recently reaffirmed its devotion to fine dining, dancing and romance. Every night from 7:30 until midnight, live music sets a celebratory mood on the dance floor. ♦ New Chef Michel Blanchet, formerly of L'Ermitage, has created a dazzling menu that matches the restaurant's renewed vigor. His five-course "Menu Gastronomique" is a great value at $47.50 and a wonderful way to taste his virtuosity. A rooftop open-air patio, available for private receptions, allows guests to enjoy Champagne at sunset against a gorgeous Beverly Hills and Century City panorama.

**AVERAGE DINNER FOR TWO: $80**
DOES NOT INCLUDE WINE, TAX AND GRATUITY

ITALIAN
FREQUENT DINING & GIVING PROGRAM

# LOCANDA VENETA

8638 WEST THIRD STREET
LOS ANGELES, CA 90048
(310) 274-1893
*Visa & Major Credit Cards*
*Dinner Mon–Sat * Lunch Mon–Fri*

*Proprietor*
JEAN-LOUIS DE MORI

*Chef/Proprietor*
ANTONIO TOMMASI
*Chef*
MASSIMO ORMANI

## Menu Highlights

❦

*Appetizers*
RADICCHIO LETTUCE SALAD
• THIN SLICES OF RAW BEEF
WITH PARMESAN & ARUGULA IN
BALSAMIC VINEGAR DRESSING

*Entrées*
TRIANGLE RAVIOLI FILLED
WITH LOBSTER IN A
CREAMY SAFFRON SAUCE
• POTATO DUMPLING WITH
CHICKEN & VEGETABLE SAUCE

DOWN A SIDE STREET IN WEST HOLLYWOOD IS A TINY EATERY causing a big commotion around town. The restaurant is Locanda Veneta, meaning Venetian inn, a homey place with cozy pastel booths and large windows that open to the street. The ambiance is unpretentious, the dining experience relaxed and intimate; the lack of hovering waiters makes for a leisurely, very European feel. ♦ Owners Jean-Louis De Mori and Antonio Tommasi are the driving force behind the restaurant. De Mori, a professional restaurateur, hails from the Italian Riviera. Tommasi, formerly of Rex, Il Ristorante and Chianti-Cucina, mans the open kitchen, emphasizing seafood, pasta and the regional cuisine of Venice. ♦ "I love that hearty regional fare, but not as a steady diet," says Tommasi. "So I've tried to lighten it up for the Southern California climate and palate." He has done it well, creating a style of cooking that connoisseurs of Italian cuisine dream of.

**AVERAGE DINNER FOR TWO: $50**
DOES NOT INCLUDE WINE, TAX AND GRATUITY

**ITALIAN**
FREQUENT DINING & GIVING PROGRAM

# L'OPERA
101 PINE AVENUE
LONG BEACH, CA 90802
(310) 491-0066

*Visa & Major Credit Cards*
*Open Daily for Dinner • Lunch Mon-Fri*

*General Manager*
ANTONIO MORETTI
*Proprietor*
ENZO DE MURO

*Executive Chef*
STEFANO COLAIACOMO

## Menu Highlights
▲▼▲

*Appetizers*
FRESH MOZZARELLA ROLLED
WITH RADICCHIO
PUFF PASTRY BAKED &
SERVED WITH MUSHROOM
SAUCE • SCALLOPS,
SHRIMP, PORCINI
& FRESH TOMATOES
IN PARCHMENT

*Entrées*
CHOICE OF FOUR PASTAS
SERVED ON A LARGE
PLATTER • GRILLED BRAIDED
LAMB FILET TOPPED WITH
BUTTER & SAGE

WHEN PARTNERS ANTONIO CAGNOLO, OWNER OF ANTONELLO Ristorante in Santa Ana, Enzo De Muro, Terry Antonelli, Frank Di Bella and David L. Maffei saw a historic, earthquake-damaged Bank of America building, they recognized an undiscovered masterpiece. Today the old bank vault houses a superb selection of wines, and the old lobby has been transformed into a sedate Roman entrance that reveals a black granite and mahogany bar flanked by Italian marble columns and small tables. ◆ An integral part of Long Beach's renaissance, L'Opera was designed by the talented Hatch Brothers. The dining room's white recessed ceiling preserves the building's original, elegant molding, and light fixtures echo turn-of-the-century lamp posts outside. Downstairs, a softly lit banquet room doubles as art gallery. ◆ Like the dining areas, Executive Chef Stefano Colaiacomo's tasty, Roman fare blends modern and classic, and his hearty pasta dishes epitomize an unpretentious approach to serious eating.

**AVERAGE DINNER FOR TWO: $50**
DOES NOT INCLUDE WINE, TAX AND GRATUITY

**FRENCH**
FREQUENT DINING & GIVING PROGRAM

# L'ORANGERIE

903 NORTH LA CIENEGA BOULEVARD
LOS ANGELES, CA 90069
(310) 652-9770
*Visa & Major Credit Cards*
*Dinner Tues–Sun • Lunch Tues–Fri*

*Maître d'*
ALBERT CHARBONNEAU

*Chef*
JEAN-CLAUDE
PARACHINI

## Menu Highlights

*Appetizers*
EGGS IN THE SHELL WITH
CAVIAR • PRAWN SALAD WITH
FRESH GREEN BEANS &
ARTICHOKE, BASIL & LEMON
DRESSING

*Entrées*
SALMON COOKED IN CLAY
WITH SPINACH & OLIVE OIL
• ROASTED RACK OF LAMB WITH
DIJON & THYME, POMMES
SOUFFLÉES • MAINE LOBSTER
FRICASSÉE WITH ROASTED
POTATOES & GARLIC

TRUE TO ITS ORIGINS, L'ORANGERIE IS AS UNCOMPROMISINGLY French in its cuisine as it is in its design. A romantic new outdoor terrace leads to the restaurant's arched doorway, which is flanked by clipped orange trees and a formal parterre of boxwood that looks like a miniature garden in Versailles. Inside, Louis XIV furnishings, antique paintings and orange-hued linens dress the luminous dining room. ♦ L'Orangerie is a successful recreation of Gerard and Virginia Ferry's namesake restaurant in Paris. From ambiance to entrées, it nurtures and pampers the senses. Soft piano music four nights a week and a seasonal all-vegetable lunch add to L'Orangerie's attractions. ♦ To keep the kitchen's competitive edge, Chef Jean-Claude Parachini has joined forces with Gerard Ferry. With three-star L'Ambroisie of Paris on his resumé, Parachini creates what Ferry calls "enlightened cuisine," an exciting, original cooking style in step with the '90s.

**AVERAGE DINNER FOR TWO: $100**
DOES NOT INCLUDE WINE, TAX AND GRATUITY

WE'D LIKE TO SHAKE UP *your* IDEA OF A MARTINI.

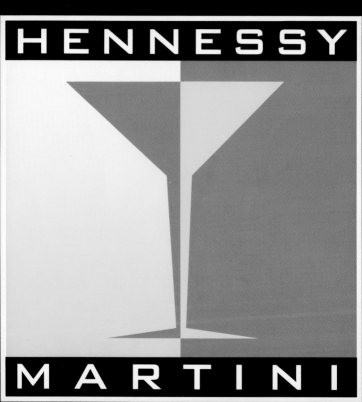

HENNESSY

MARTINI

# *Proper attire for a night on the town.*

Planche n° 5 - **LA BOUTEILLE** -

**MEDITERRANEAN**
FREQUENT DINING & GIVING PROGRAM

# LUMA

1323 MONTANA AVENUE
AT EUCLID AVENUE
SANTA MONICA, CA 90403
(310) 451-0900

*Visa & Major Credit Cards*
*Open Daily for Dinner • Lunch Mon–Fri*

*Proprietor*
GINO DIAFERIA

*Chef/Proprietor*
ERIC STAPELMAN

## Menu Highlights

*Appetizers*
GRILLED PORTOBELLO
MUSHROOMS WITH POTATO
ZUCCHINI GALETTE
• SEA VEGETABLE &
ASIAN FIELD GREENS
• LUMA VERDE WITH 16
VARIETIES OF WILD BABY GREENS

*Entrées*
SPICY MEXICAN FISH SOUP WITH
RED SNAPPER & CORN MASA
• GRILLED BIG EYE TUNA
WITH FENNEL SALAD &
PEPPERONATA SAUCE
• GRILLED SALMON WITH
SPRING SUCCOTASH

LUMA, THE NEW YORK RESTAURANT THAT HAS WON RAVE REVIEWS from *Gourmet, Details* and *The New York Times,* along with accolades from the entertainment community, has now made its way to Santa Monica's Montana Avenue. Chef/proprietor Eric Stapelman and Chef Robert Smith have taken their seasonal fare to health-conscious Southern Californians. They adhere to a firm commitment to use only the finest ingredients featuring organic produce, farm-raised fish and free-range poultry. ♦ One of the most unique aspects of Luma is that it is a gourmet restaurant for people who care about what they eat. The menu offers delectable dishes prepared without sugar or dairy products. Wild and cultivated greens and vegetables, along with fresh fish and fowl, are accompanied by freshly baked breads topped with Luma's signature spreads. Memorable examples are the lima bean and garlic blend, lentil and shrimp, and pumpkin flavors. ♦ The elegant dining room, designed by Cheryl Brantner and Richard Espinet, is ideal for business, luncheons and social dinners alike.

**AVERAGE DINNER FOR TWO: $60**
DOES NOT INCLUDE WINE, TAX AND GRATUITY

# LUNARIA

10351 SANTA MONICA BOULEVARD
LOS ANGELES, CA 90025
(310) 282-8870

*Visa & Major Credit Cards*

*Dinner Tues–Sat • Lunch Tues–Fri*

*Proprietor*
EDWIGE JACOUPY

*Proprietor*
BERNARD JACOUPY

## Menu Highlights

### Appetizers

COLD SOUP OF FRESH TOMA-
TOES, CUCUMBERS, BELLPEPPERS
& TOASTED ALMOND • SEARED
SEA SCALLOPS ON GREEN LENTILS
"DU PUY," BACON VINAIGRETTE
• SEVEN-HOUR LEG OF LAMB
RAVIOLI IN RED WINE SAUCE

### Entrées

ROASTED MONKFISH WITH
BARIGOULE OF ARTICHOKES &
ROCK SHRIMPS • GRATIN OF
SEABASS PROVENÇAL • SMOKED
HALIBUT WITH LEMON-PEPPER
LINGUINI & BURGUNDY BUTTER

NAMED AFTER AN OLD-FASHIONED YET UNUSUAL WHITE GARDEN flower, Lunaria serves a unique combination of piping hot jazz and uncomplicated California/French fare in its casually elegant lounge and dining room. Under the guidance of Chef Jean-Pierre Bosc, a rising culinary star in Los Angeles, Lunaria's kitchen demonstrates a unique cooking style that combines the lightness of Provençal cuisine with the earthy flavors of his native Lyon. Bosc's credentials include Paul Bocuse in France and Fennel in Los Angeles, and his sassy, innovative dishes match the vitality of the music. Lunaria's reputation for good jazz attracts serious musicians from the music industry who come here to play or to listen to their peers perform. ♦ Unlike many modern restaurants, this one evokes a subdued and soothing warmth that invites diners to linger. Soft pastels, rattan bistro chairs and flattering rosy lighting contribute to the overall calm and cozy effect. The owner's flair for creative decor and attention to detail even extends to the hand-painted dinner plates and to a wonderful collection of original Impressionist paintings.

**AVERAGE DINNER FOR TWO: $49**
DOES NOT INCLUDE WINE, TAX AND GRATUITY

**FRENCH**
FREQUENT DINING & GIVING PROGRAM

# MA MAISON

HOTEL SOFITEL
8555 BEVERLY BOULEVARD
LOS ANGELES, CA 90048
(213) 655-1991
*Visa & Major Credit Cards*
*Dinner Tues-Sat • Lunch Tues-Fri*

| *Maître d'* | *Chef* |
|---|---|
| J.B. TORCHON | MARKUS SCHAEDLER |

## Menu Highlights
❦

*Appetizers*
SAUTÉED SHRIMP ON A BED OF
COUSCOUS WITH PINK CURRY
SAUCE • FRESHLY SEARED
TUNA ON MIXED GREENS WITH
CREAMY SESAME VINAIGRETTE
• FOIE GRAS OVER FRESH ASPIC

*Entrées*
BROILED DOVER SOLE WITH
CAPER LEMON SAUCE, ASPARAGUS
& PARSLEY POTATOES • MAINE
LOBSTER WITH BUTTER SAUCE
• OVEN-CRISPED BREAST OF
DUCK WITH MANGO
PEPPER SAUCE

KNOWN FOR ITS ORIGINALITY, MA MAISON CONTINUES TO FLOUR-
ish as one of Los Angeles' finest restaurants. Once a haven for such luminaries as Orson Welles, Ma Maison is still a celebrity favorite. Maître d'
J.B. Torchon greets every guest at the door to ensure that all receive star
treatment. ♦ The atmosphere is casually elegant. In the daytime, the
restaurant is bright, airy and gardenlike; by night, Tiffany-lit ficus trees
reach toward a slide-open skylight, revealing the heavens for a touch of
romance. ♦ The restaurant's cuisine comes to life in a spacious kitchen visible beyond the bar. Under the supervision of Austrian-born Chef Markus
Schaedler, Ma Maison's perfectly balanced menu with distinct French flair
is a perfect match to the restaurant's casual and friendly atmosphere.

**AVERAGE DINNER FOR TWO: $70**
DOES NOT INCLUDE WINE, TAX AND GRATUITY

# McCormick & Schmick's

600 Hope Place
Los Angeles, CA 90071
(213) 629-1929
*Visa & Major Credit Cards*
*Open Daily for Dinner • Lunch Mon–Sat*

General Manager
SCOTT SMITH

Executive Chef
ANDREW CATTANEO

## Menu Highlights

*Appetizers*
DUNGENESS CRABCAKES
• ROCK SHRIMP POPCORN
• PEPPER-SEARED AHI WITH
ASIAN CUCUMBER SALAD
• PENN COVE MUSSELS

*Entrées*
GRILLED CALIFORNIA SWORD-
FISH WITH PESTO & WILD RICE
• HAWAIIAN AHI
"BLACK & BLUE" WITH WASABI
• OVEN-ROASTED SEA BASS WITH
DUNGENESS CRAB & BRIE

EVERY MORNING CHEF ANDREW CATTANEO EXAMINES THE FRESH seafood that is flown in from ports across the U.S., including McCormick & Schmick's own Portland fish company located next to their flagship restaurant. Bringing the flavors of the Pacific Northwest to downtown Los Angeles is a bit cumbersome but well worth the effort. Twenty seafood selections appear on the menu, including a variety of oysters farmed from bays in the upper Pacific Rim. Says Proprietor Doug Schmick, "The end result of our diligence is a menu filled with classic, mostly American seafood." In short, he's created a restaurant that puts the catch of a nation on its tables. Noteworthy are the cedar planked salmon cooked American Indian fashion over a splinter of oiled cedar, and the Pacific seafood stew with mussels, prawns, clams and crab in a red wine sauce. ♦ Beveled glass and dark wood contribute to the clubby atmosphere, along with a bar that features twenty-five single malt scotches and ten micro-breweries. It appears the decor was chosen to highlight tradition over trend, much like the menu.

**AVERAGE DINNER FOR TWO: $50**
DOES NOT INCLUDE WINE, TAX AND GRATUITY

# MICHAEL'S

1147 THIRD STREET
SANTA MONICA, CA 90403
(310) 451-0843

*Visa & Major Credit Cards*
*Dinner Tues-Sat • Lunch Tues-Fri*

*Proprietor*
MICHAEL McCARTY

*Manager*
HARVEY FRIEND
*Chef*
WENDY ROSKIN

### Menu Highlights

*Appetizers*
SPAGHETTINI WITH NORWEGIAN SALMON, CHARDONNAY CREAM SAUCE, ROASTED RED & YELLOW PEPPERS, BABY ASPARAGUS & CRYSTAL LAKE SALMON CAVIAR

*Entrées*
SHELTON CHICKEN & MONTRACHET GOAT CHEESE WITH ROASTED RED & YELLOW PEPPERS, MAUI ONIONS & CILANTRO

• CALIFORNIA PRIME LAMB SADDLE WITH DOUBLE-BLANCHED GARLIC, PINE NUTS & FRESH BASIL

NOW 40, MICHAEL McCARTY IS STILL CONSIDERED SOMETHING OF a boy wonder. At 18, he opened his first restaurant in Paris, where he graduated from the Ecole Hôtelière de Paris, the Cordon Bleu and the Academie du Vin. Back in the United States, he completed a program at Cornell University, then went to the University of Colorado at Boulder, where he taught French cooking, earned a business degree and opened his second restaurant. ♦ At the age of 25, McCarty put it all together and opened Michael's in Santa Monica. Combining his classical French training with his American background, he is now known as one of the pioneers of California cuisine. ♦ McCarty, one of the first restaurateurs to showcase modern art, believes that his clientele appreciates both great art and fine cuisine. With the quality of his collection (Jasper Johns, Richard Diebenkorn and David Hockney, among others) and the distinctiveness of his menu, that assumption is easy to support.

**AVERAGE DINNER FOR TWO: $70**
DOES NOT INCLUDE WINE, TAX AND GRATUITY

# MATSUHISA

129 N. LA CIENEGA BLVD.
BEVERLY HILLS, CA 90211
(310) 659-9639

*Visa & Major Credit Cards*
*Open Daily for Dinner • Lunch Mon-Fri*

*Beverage Manager*
YUICHI SAITO

*Chef/Proprietor*
NOBU MATSUHISA

*Manager*
MICHAEL HIDE
CARDENAS

## Menu Highlights

*Appetizers*
SHRIMP TEMPURA HAND ROLL
WITH FRIED PRAWNS, ASPARAGUS
& CREAM SAUCE, KELP ROLL
• SLIPPER LOBSTER WITH PEPPER
SAUCE • VARIETY OF TEMPURAS
MADE WITH PUMPKINS, ENOKI
MUSHROOMS, SNOW PEAS &
SWEET POTATO

*Entrées*
NEW-STYLE SASHIMI: SLICED
HALIBUT FILET, SESAME SEEDS,
SOY, GINGER & GARLIC SAUTÉED
IN OLIVE OIL • TIGER SHRIMP
SAUTÉED WITH SHIITAKES,
WASABI PEPPER SAUCE

ON BEST RESTAURANT LISTS AROUND THE WORLD, SIX-YEAR-OLD Matsuhisa is a petite restaurant consisting of only seventy seats. They are constantly filled with luminaries who come in droves to sample dishes made by the "high priest of seafood," Chef/owner Nobuyuki Matsuhisa. His last name means evergreen and his menu is ever blossoming with delicacies from the sea. Highly recommended is the Chef's Choice menu "Omakase," the most exotic and delicious dishes of the day personally selected by Matsuhisa. A great value at $60, it allows the chef to be creative with seven to twelve courses and guests to experience his virtuosity and range. ♦ Time spent in kitchens in South America has given Matsuhisa a unique way with spices and chilies, the dominant flavors in his most popular dishes. "Food is my life. I love to cook, I love to handle fish, I love to eat," enthuses Matsuhisa. "You could say my cuisine is seafood with heart."

**AVERAGE DINNER FOR TWO: $80**
DOES NOT INCLUDE WINE, TAX AND GRATUITY

# OPUS

2425 WEST OLYMPIC BOULEVARD
AT 26TH ST.
SANTA MONICA, CA 90404
(310) 829-2112
*Visa & Major Credit Cards*
*Open Daily for Dinner • Lunch Mon-Fri*

*Proprietor*
CHARLES ALMOND

*Chef*
IAN WINSLADE

## Menu Highlights

*Appetizers*
SEARED TUNA WITH
WARM COUSCOUS SALAD
• SALMON TARTARE WITH
GRATED HORSERADISH
• DUNGENESS CRABMEAT WITH
TRUFFLES & POTATO SALAD
• SHRIMP & SCALLOP RAVIOLI

*Entrées*
STRIPED BASS WITH
HERB-MARINATED WHITE BEANS
• CRISPED RED SNAPPER,
ROASTED GARLIC & SHIITAKES
• SEARED MAINE SCALLOPS
WITH APPLES & SAGE
• POT-ROASTED RABBIT WITH
POTATOES & BRUSSEL SPROUTS

ENTERING OPUS IS LIKE STROLLING INTO THE GRAND SALON OF an ocean liner. Spacious and elegant with pearwood and glass as far as the eye can see, the interior is stunning enough visually to compete with the restaurant's sumptuous menu. ♦ Chef Ian Winslade, formerly of Le Bernardin in New York and not yet thirty, emphasizes seafood specialties made with fine ingredients that he seeks out with an unrelenting passion. Salmon steaks are oven-roasted in a shellfish sauce and finished with basil; the mahi-mahi is delicately poached in a spicy broth with celery and fried leeks. ♦ Wanting an irresitable location for Opus, Proprietor Charles Almond chose the lovely Santa Monica Water Garden complex. During summer months, the restaurant's patio is a wonderful spot to watch the surrounding fountains bedazzle in the California sun. At night, the curved bar area inside doubles as a bistro where diners can sample moderately priced, seasonal fare. The wine list here, and in the main dining room, contains a large selection of excellent California, French and German vintages.

**AVERAGE DINNER FOR TWO: $70**
DOES NOT INCLUDE WINE, TAX AND GRATUITY

# ORLEANS

11705 NATIONAL BOULEVARD
LOS ANGELES, CA 90064
(310) 479-4187

*Major Credit Cards*
*Dinner Mon-Sat • Lunch Mon-Fri*

*Proprietor*              *Chefs*
MARY ATKINSON      GUSTAVO BRAMBILA
                                RAUL CONTRERAS

**Menu Highlights**

*Appetizers*
CAJUN POPCORN
(CRABMEAT, CRAWFISH &
ALLIGATOR) LIGHTLY
DEEP-FRIED & SERVED
WITH SHERRY*
SAUCE • CHICKEN GUMBO
WITH ANDOUILLE SAUSAGE

*Entrées*
BROILED SWORDFISH
WITH HOT FANNY SAUCE
• BLACKENED PRIME
RIB WITH BROWNED
GARLIC BUTTER
• BLACKENED FISH

ORLEANS IS ONE OF THE FEW CREOLE-CAJUN RESTAURANTS TO survive the hot spice and "blackened everything" trend. It brings to Cajun cuisine what the deep South delivers in hospitality. ♦ A superb Cajun menu served in an airy, slightly funky atmosphere draws a crowd of both regulars and fun-seeking adventurers. Homemade jalapeño cheese rolls and tangy crabmeat popcorn make sensational starters, and the savory blackened prime rib with browned garlic butter is irresistible. ♦ As you enter this stately mansion-style eatery, the Southern hospitality is unmistakable. Orleans' pedigree is flawless. Original cuisine consultant and Cajun master Paul Prudhomme, and owner Mary Atkinson created what is now a mecca for diners who enjoy dishes prepared with zing and sass. Orleans accents authenticity with a fervor for freshness — you won't find a freezer on these premises.

**AVERAGE DINNER FOR TWO: $50**
DOES NOT INCLUDE WINE, TAX AND GRATUITY

# PARKWAY GRILL

510 SOUTH ARROYO PARKWAY
PASADENA, CA 91105
(818) 795-1001

*Visa & Major Credit Cards*
*Open Daily for Dinner • Lunch Sun-Fri*

*Proprietors*
**BOB SMITH**
**GREGG SMITH**

*Chef*
**HUGO MOLINA**

## Menu Highlights

*Appetizers*

CHARRED RARE PEPPERED
TUNA WITH CUCUMBER
SALAD & SOY VINAIGRETTE
• LOBSTER COCOA CRÊPE IN
SUNDRIED TOMATO CREAM

*Entrées*

SONOMA BABY LAMB • GRILLED
SWORDFISH WITH SAFFRON
RISOTTO, FENNEL ARTICHOKE
BRUNOISE & OLIVE-ROASTED
PEPPER & MINT RELISH
• WHOLE FRIED CATFISH WITH
FRESH GINGER SCALLIONS &
LIME SOY SAUCE

IN THE CENTER OF OLD PASADENA IS ONE OF THE MOST POPULAR restaurants on the east side of Los Angeles County, the Parkway Grill. Brothers Gregg and Bob Smith opened the restaurant eight years ago, catering to Pasadena businessmen at lunch and a bustling after-theatre crowd at night. ♦ A 1920s brick building with large skylights and towering ficus trees sets the scene for the Parkway Grill's healthy California cuisine. Chef Hugo Molina emphasizes freshness and seeks out purveyors who will provide produce and meats to his specifications, and the restaurant's own organic garden provides exotic greens and vegetables. ♦ "We search the nation for these products," says Gregg Smith. "They may be expensive, but they're the best we can find. Our customers are more adventuresome than ever in the past, so we prepare dishes that are difficult to make at home." ♦ Updating American regional cuisine, Chef Molina's dishes combine new tastes with stringent requirements — nothing comes from a can or freezer except the extra-virgin oil and the homemade ice cream.

**AVERAGE DINNER FOR TWO: $50**
DOES NOT INCLUDE WINE, TAX AND GRATUITY

# PATINA

5955 MELROSE AVENUE
LOS ANGELES, CA 90038
(213) 467-1108

*Visa & Major Credit Cards*
*Open Daily for Dinner • Lunch Tues-Fri*

*Proprietor*
CHRISTINE SPLICHAL

*Chef/Proprietor*
JOACHIM SPLICHAL

## Menu Highlights

*Appetizers*

POTATO ROLL OF SCALLOPS WITH
BROWN BUTTER VINAIGRETTE
• SANDWICH OF CORN BLINIS
WITH MARINATED SALMON
• SANTA BARBARA SHRIMP
WITH MASHED POTATOES &
POTATO TRUFFLE CHIPS

*Entrées*

GRATIN OF LAMB WITH
MASHED POTATOES &
GARLIC • PEPPERED TOURNEDOS
OF TUNA WITH CHINESE
VEGETABLES & PONZU
SAUCE • JOHN DORY WITH
CALF'S FEET & OYSTERS

MASTER CHEF JOACHIM SPLICHAL'S HOLLYWOOD ESTABLISHMENT sits on the hallowed site of the renowned Le St. Germain. Like its predecessor, Patina is quiet, private and small, but similarities end there. With his wife and manager, Christine, Chef Splichal has created a restaurant that is dramatic yet comfortable, a place where each guest receives the owners' personal touch. ◆ Patina's decor fuses minimalist and classic details. Copper sconce lighting, mixed-tone woods, silk fabrics and elegant place settings stand out against creamy white walls. Elegantly attired by Hugo Boss, the waiters offer maximum personal service. ◆ Patina's style reflects Chef Splichal's tasty, uncluttered cuisine. Built around wholesome foods, his menu offers two reasonable prix-fixe meals as well as à la carte selections. "We have designed a menu for the 1990s," he says. "It is fresh, light and original in design."

**AVERAGE DINNER FOR TWO: $85**
DOES NOT INCLUDE WINE, TAX AND GRATUITY

# PAZZIA/FENNEL

755 NORTH LA CIENEGA BOULEVARD
LOS ANGELES, CA 90069
(310) 657-9271 (PAZZIA)
(310) 657-8787 (FENNEL)

*Visa & Major Credit Cards*
*Dinner Mon–Sat • Lunch Tues–Sat*

*General Manager*
JEAN-CHRISTOPHE
LA VARRAT

*Chef*
ENRICO TROVA

## Menu Highlights

*Appetizers*
ITALIAN CRABCAKES
• CARPACCIO OF TUNA
• GOAT CHEESE SALAD

*Entrées*
SPAGHETTI WITH
LANGOUSTINE & BROCCOLI
• VEAL CHOP CACCIATORE
• GRILLED SALMON
WITH PESTO SAUCE
• ROTISSERIE CHICKEN
• NEW YORK STEAK & FRIES
WITH PEPPERCORN SAUCE

SINCE ITS OPENING FIVE YEARS AGO, PAZZIA HAS BEEN SERVING excellent Northern Italian cuisine including the finest thin crusted pizzas and fresh pastas in town. Now under the direction of Chef Enrico Trova, the restaurant's kitchen continues to produce fresh, innovative dishes that keep customers returning for more. ♦ Pazzia's Italian appeal commences on the terrace, where diners gather to begin and end their evening with a drink. Across the terrace is a gelateria that serves sinful ice creams mixed by hand the old-fashioned way. Inside, every detail of the dining room, from the glass wall that fills the high-ceilinged space with light to the sleek open-to-view kitchen, is evidence of the management's perfectionism. As the first authentic "bistrot" to open in Los Angeles, Fennel is a classic example of a "Parisian neighborhood restaurant," where the atmosphere is warm, the food is like home cooking and prices are attractive for every day dining. Jean-Christophe La Varrat and his staff make sure you have a memorable bistrot dining experience without even getting on a plane to Paris.

**AVERAGE DINNER FOR TWO: $80**
DOES NOT INCLUDE WINE, TAX AND GRATUITY

# PINOT

12969 VENTURA BLVD.
AT COLDWATER CANYON
STUDIO CITY, CA 91604
(818) 990-0500

*Visa & Major Credit Cards*
*Open Daily for Dinner • Lunch Mon–Fri • Sunday Brunch*

*General Manager*
DOUGLAS R. FLOHR

*Executive Chef*
OCTAVIO BECERRA

## Menu Highlights

*Appetizers*

CARAMELIZED ONION TART
WITH MARINATED SALMON &
CREAM • SAUTÉED SCALLOPS
WITH PORCINI & BABY
ARTICHOKE RAGOUT

*Entrées*

RAVIOLI DE NICE: STUFFED
WITH BEEF FILLING & SERVED
WITH RED WINE SAUCE
• ROASTED DUCK CONFIT
WITH SCALLIONS & WHITE
MUSHROOMS WITH RIESLING
• WHITEFISH WITH BRANDADE &
ROASTED GARLIC SAUCE

JOACHIM SPLICHAL HAS SLOWLY BUT SURELY BEEN CHANGING THE face of dining in Los Angeles. First it was the flawless Patina. Now it's his new Studio City venture that brings some of the most innovative and classic dining experiences to the South Land. ♦ Executive Chef Octavio Becerra spent a year studying in the French and Basque kitchens of Europe, absorbing not only the cuisine, but the culture that is so dedicated to bistro fare. One bite of his namesake appetizer, Farinette, lets you know this is the start of something big, the bread filling and smoky chicken covered by braised mushrooms a dream. "Everything revolves around the table," says Becerra pointing to his straightforward menu and collection of photos and postcards from Europe that surround the tables. ♦ End the night with a sumptuous chocolate crème brulée for the complete French bistro treatment.

**AVERAGE DINNER FOR TWO: $60**
DOES NOT INCLUDE WINE, TAX AND GRATUITY

# POSTO

14928 VENTURA BLVD.
AT KESTER AVENUE
SHERMAN OAKS, CA 91403
(818) 784-4400

*Visa & Major Credit Cards*
*Open Daily for Dinner 8 Lunch Mon-Fri*

*Manager*
NINO BATTAGLIA

*Chef*
LUCIANO PELLEGRINI

## Menu Listings

*Appetizers*
SNAILS IN PANCETTA WITH
POLENTA ON A BED OF GARLIC
AND SPINACH • WARM SCALLOPS
WITH SWEET PEPPERS &
SICILIAN CAPERS • AHI
CARPACCIO WITH CAPONATA

*Entrées*
LAMB CHOPS WITH HERB
INFUSION • ROASTED VEAL WITH
PORCINI • AN ASSORTMENT OF
HOUSEMADE SAUSAGES,
INCLUDING WILD BOAR,
VENISON AND LAMB

OWNER PIERO SELVAGGIO FEELS HIS LATEST VENTURE COMPLETES a Los Angeles restaurant trilogy that began with Valentino in the 70s. Capturing the elegance of the time, Valentino was soon followed by Primi, synonymous with 80s style. His finale, at least for now, is Posto, a restaurant that heralds the 90s with a modest, back-to-basics culinary attitude. ♦ Selvaggio, determined to come up with a traditional rustic menu, sent Chef Luciano Pellegrini to a Fruili mountain trattoria for three months to study the art of *Focolar,* the preparation of family-style dishes cooked on an open hearth. The results are country dishes that were overlooked in the past. *Ribollita,* a thick reboiled Tuscan soup, and *brasato al Barolo,* a robust, wine-laced beef stew, warm anyone coming in from the cold. ♦ Says Selvaggio, "Traditionally, cuisine in the trattoria is 'Mama's cooking' and I believe that Posto offers food that is equal in simplicity and substance." It is fitting that Posto's kitchen, like the heart of any family, is given its due as the restaurant's focal point, surrounded by sensual rooms designed by Roman architect Osvaldo Maiozzi.

**AVERAGE DINNER FOR TWO: $55**
DOES NOT INCLUDE WINE, TAX AND GRATUITY

# PRIMI

10543 PICO BOULEVARD
WEST LOS ANGELES, CA 90064
(310) 475-9235

*Visa & Major Credit Cards*
*Dinner Mon–Sat• Lunch Mon-Fri*

| *Manager* | *Chef* |
|---|---|
| DONATO POTO | ENRICO GLAUDO |

## Menu Highlights

*Appetizers*
GRILLED EGGPLANT WITH
OLIVES & PEPPERS
• DUCKLING CRÊPE
WITH CREMONA MUSTARD
• BLACK GARGANELLI
WITH ROCK SHRIMP
& TOMATO

*Entrées*
RISOTTO WITH ASPARAGUS &
TRUFFLE FONDUTA • GRILLED
WHITEFISH WITH SAFFRON SAUCE
• ROASTED VEAL LOIN WITH
SAGE & CHARDONNAY SAUCE

PRIMI, WHICH MEANS "FIRST PLATES" IN ITALIAN, PROUDLY proclaims itself as "a restaurant of starts and finishes." If sampling a selection of exquisitely prepared appetizers and "mini" portions seems exciting, then Primi is the place. ♦ Launched by restaurateur Piero Selvaggio, who also owns the famed Valentino Restaurant, Primi's innovative "grazing" concept was an immediate hit with local patrons, who have kept the restaurant hopping for both lunch and dinner. A polished black lacquer bar and spacious open kitchen dominate the casual dining room, which showcases the imaginative, art-inspired cuisine. ♦ Aside from "first plates," Chef Enrico Glaudo also offers something larger for heartier appetites. Examples are the baked *branzino* and potatoes with Italian herbs and roasted rabbit, served with a sweet pepper and olive sauce. His dishes sing with flavor and make an imprint that is difficult to erase.

**AVERAGE DINNER FOR TWO: $60**
DOES NOT INCLUDE WINE, TAX AND GRATUITY

*Introducing*

# BAILEYS LIGHT™

*33% fewer calories, 50% less fat, 100% delicious*

*Add some sparkle to your meals.*

★
**S. PELLEGRINO**

*Sparkling Natural Mineral Water*
*Bottled at the Source, San Pellegrino, Italy.*
*Since 1899.*

# REMI

1451 THIRD STREET PROMENADE
SANTA MONICA, CA 90401
(310) 393-6545

*Visa & Major Credit Cards*
*Open Daily • Lunch & Dinner*

*General Manager*
CLAUDIO BONOTTO
*Co-Proprietor*
JIVAN TABIBIAN

*Chef*
JOSIE LEBALCH

## Menu Highlights

*Appetizers*

SMOKED GOOSE PROSCIUTTO
WITH FRESH GREENS

• SEA SCALLOPS MARINATED
WITH PROSECCO VINAIGRETTE,
SERVED WITH CANELLINI
BEANS & ROSEMARY

*Entrées*

ROASTED RED SNAPPER IN
ONION & ORANGE VINEGAR,
WITH PIGNOLIAS & RAISINS

• RAVIOLI FILLED WITH FRESH
TUNA, GINGER & LIGHT
TOMATO SAUCE • WOOD-
GRILLED FREE RANGE
CORNISH HEN MARINATED
WITH HERBS

REMI BRINGS TO MIND THE NORTHWEST ADRIATIC, WHERE lagoons and tidal channels encircle the small islands of Venice. Translated from Italian, Remi means gondola oars, and co-owner/designer Adam Tihany's interpretation is a nautical medley of blond wood, wide plank floors and blue-and-white-striped banquettes that evoke Venetian boathouses. In the center of the airy, white interior, accented by bright red and yellow wall sconces, is a grappa cart loaded with more than seventy selections. ♦ "We are a trattoria," says partner Jivan Tabibian, "and offer a return to a simple dining experience." This refreshing idea is reiterated in the breezy sidewalk patio, with its rattan chairs, canvas umbrellas, windswept blue awnings and Santa Monica sunlight. Here, Chef Josie LeBalch recreates the Venetian-inspired fare conceived by Executive Chef Francesco Antonucci that celebrates the fresh, basic ingredients of the Veneto.

**AVERAGE DINNER FOR TWO: $60**
DOES NOT INCLUDE WINE TAX AND GRATUITY

# REX, IL RISTORANTE

617 SOUTH OLIVE STREET
LOS ANGELES, CA 90014
(213) 627-2300

*Visa & Major Credit Cards*
*Dinner Mon-Sat • Lunch Thurs & Fri*

| Manager | Chef |
|---------|------|
| DANILO TERRIBILI | ODETTA SADA |

## Menu Highlights

*Appetizers*

BREAST OF CHICKEN
FOIE GRAS • RUCOLA
SALAD, WITH RAISINS,
WALNUTS & ORATA
• PAPPARDELLE WITH
QUAIL & ARTICHOKES

*Entrées*

SALMON WITH YELLOW BELL
PEPPER, BLACK TRUFFLE
& VEGETABLES • GRILLED
ORATA & SALMORIGLIO
WITH POTATOES &
OREGANO • VEAL
CHOP WITH ROSEMARY
SAUCE & BLACK TRUFFLE

FOR AN UNFORGETTABLE ITALIAN MEAL, STEP ON BOARD THE most elegant "luxury liner" in Los Angeles, Rex, Il Ristorante. The restaurant has earned an international reputation for its cuisine and unusual ambiance. ♦ Proprietor Mauro Vincenti recreated the 1930s interior of an opulent cruise ship and docked it in the Art Deco Oviatt Building with its marble, neo-Gothic woodwork and Lalique glass. His remodel is so convincing that you almost expect to find Clark Gable or Myrna Loy seated next to you. ♦ Credited with bringing Italian *nuova cucina* to Los Angeles, Vincenti is both pioneer and perfectionist. The massive two-story kitchen is spacious enough to hold the large Italian staff, but doesn't have room for a freezer, since Vincenti insists on complete freshness and no pre-cooking. ♦ In a world of sparse style and shortcuts on quality, dining at Rex, Il Ristorante brings back luxury, pleasure and plenitude.

**AVERAGE DINNER FOR TWO: $100**
DOES NOT INCLUDE WINE, TAX AND GRATUITY

**FRENCH/CALIFORNIA**
FREQUENT DINING & GIVING PROGRAM

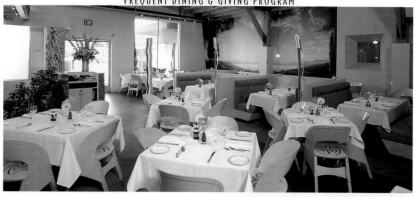

# RÖCKENWAGNER

2435 MAIN STREET
SANTA MONICA, CA 90405
(310) 399-6504

*Visa & Major Credit Cards*
*Open Daily • Lunch & Dinner*

*Proprietor*
MARY RÖCKENWAGNER

*Chef/Proprietor*
HANS RÖCKENWAGNER
*Chef*
TREY FOSHEE

## Menu Highlights

*Appetizers*
CRAB SOUFFLÉ WITH
SLICED PAPAYA & LOBSTER
BUTTER SAUCE • SHORT STACK
OF SMOKED SALMON, POTATO
CHIPS, CRÈME FRAÎCHE &
CAVIAR • NAPOLEON OF
DUCK FOIE GRAS

*Entrées*
TIAN OF LAMB, THINLY SLICED
ROASTED LOIN ON LAYERS OF
SPINACH, MUSHROOMS &
TOMATOES CONCASSE WITH
PROVENÇAL SAUCE • POTATO-
WRAPPED CHICKEN BREAST
STUFFED WITH MUSHROOM
DUXELLE, BRAISED LEEKS

HANS AND MARY RÖCKENWAGNER BURST ONTO THE LOS ANGELES scene eight years ago with their immensely popular and well-reviewed restaurant in Venice. They've since moved to Ocean Park in Santa Monica where they created a stunning room featuring a mural by Richard Kriegler and a courtyard designed by Frank Gehry. ♦ A native of Germany, Hans brings an inventive knack for eclectic combinations of color, flavor and texture to the Westside. His pork tenderloin served with caramelized apples topped with goat cheese, and herb-crusted tuna cooked in rice paper are two good examples. Desserts include a delicious warm chocolate tart with a liquid chocolate center served with hazelnut parfait and coffee crème anglaise. A real bakery, not a pastry shop, on the premises specializes in a variety of fresh pretzels, Rudolf Steiner health bread and many breakfast rolls. ♦ Thanks to Manager Yves Briee, the service is impeccable.

**AVERAGE DINNER FOR TWO: $60**
DOES NOT INCLUDE WINE, TAX AND GRATUITY

CALIFORNIA
FREQUENT DINING & GIVING PROGRAM

# ROXXI

1065 EAST GREEN STREET
AT WILSON AVENUE
PASADENA, CA 91106
(818) 449-4519

*Visa & Major Credit Cards*
*Open Daily for Dinner • Lunch Mon–Fri*

*Proprietors*
PATRICK & SHARON
WESTMORELAND

*Executive Chef*
JAMES HARRINGER

## Menu Highlights

*Appetizers*
DUCK RAVIOLI WITH
SHIITAKE MUSHROOMS &
SUNDRIED CRANBERRIES
• CRABCAKES WITH CREOLE
MUSTARD SAUCE

*Entrées*
THAI CURRY CHICKEN ON
RED PEPPER LINGUINI IN SPICY
PEANUT-COCONUT SAUCE
• GRILLED AHI TUNA WITH
PINEAPPLE SALSA, DAIKON
SPROUTS & SESAME BLACK BEANS

WHEN SHARON AND PATRICK WESTMORELAND OPENED THEIR California grill in a quiet storefront in sunny Pasadena, the ensuing notoriety forced them to expand into two more storefronts to handle the crowd. Serving equally healthy portions of good food and hospitality, Roxxi, tastefully decorated in a contemporary western style, features a wide range of fresh fish, fowl and game. On any given night the specials might include wild boar or venison along with traditional helpings of swordfish and salmon. The couple's signature potsticker salad and ricotta ravioli remain the most popular staples on a menu designed for serious grazing. Twelve-ounce Porterhouse cowboy steak and ranch beans, and crispy air-dried duck with papaya basil sauce are a few hearty examples. ♦ Patrick's penchant for Pacific Coast wines is evident in the superb wine list. He gives special attention to "alternative" whites (non-Chardonnays), Cabernets and, especially, Zinfandels.

**AVERAGE DINNER FOR TWO: $50**
DOES NOT INCLUDE WINE, TAX AND GRATUITY

# SPAGO

1114 HORN AVENUE
WEST HOLLYWOOD, CA 90069
(310) 652-4025

*This restaurant prefers Visa*
*Open Daily • Dinner Only*

*Proprietor*
BARBARA LAZAROFF

*Chef/Proprietor*
WOLFGANG PUCK

## Menu Highlights

*Appetizers*
SAUTÉED AMERICAN FOIE GRAS WITH SWEET & SOUR PLUM SAUCE • SAUTÉED SHRIMP CAKES WITH LIME HERB BUTTER & ROCKET SALAD

*Entrées*
SPICY FETTUCCINI WITH SAUTÉED LOBSTER IN A LOBSTER BASIL SAUCE • PIZZA WITH SPICY LOUISIANA SHRIMP, SUNDRIED TOMATOES & LEEKS • GRILLED TUNA WITH TOMATO BASIL VINAIGRETTE

THE CHEF WHO PUT CALIFORNIA CUISINE ON THE MAP, WOLFGANG Puck has a magic touch that makes Spago as alluring today as it was a decade ago when he shook the culinary world with his designer pizzas and daring food combinations. The darling of L.A.'s rich and famous, Spago has an international reputation for both its cuisine and its glamorous clientele. ◆ Once you get past the crush of photographers waiting outside for a shot of the stars, Spago is as casual as it is crowded. Puck started a trend with the first open-to-view kitchen. Barbara Lazaroff, his interior designer wife, filled the restaurant overlooking the Sunset Strip with artworks and L.A. style, then created the original decor of Puck's Chinois on Main. ◆ Born in Austria and trained in France, Puck began his stellar rise at Ma Maison. His imaginative skill has brought him super-chef status, and his talents as a food consultant are sought by restaurants around the world.

**AVERAGE DINNER FOR TWO: $70**
DOES NOT INCLUDE WINE, TAX AND GRATUITY

**AMERICAN**
FREQUENT DINING & GIVING PROGRAM

# TATOU

233 NORTH BEVERLY DRIVE
AT WILSHIRE BLVD.
BEVERLY HILLS, CA 90210
(310) 274-9955

*Visa & Major Credit Cards*
*Dinner Mon-Sat • Lunch Mon-Fri*

*Proprietor*
MARK FLEISCHMAN

*Chef*
DESI SZONNTAGH

## Menu Highlights

❖❖❖

*Appetizers*
DEVILED CRABCAKE WITH
CILANTRO MAYONNAISE &
CORN RELISH • MAINE LOBSTER
CHOWDER • POACHED
SALMON WITH ORIENTAL
CABBAGE SLAW & SEAWEED

*Entrées*
FREE-RANGE CHICKEN
WITH MUSHROOM DUXELLES &
GARLIC MASHED POTATOES
• HERB-PACKED SNAPPER
WITH OVEN-DRIED TOMATOES
• GRILLED TUNA WITH
SESAME GINGER DRESSING

MARK AND ALAN FLEISCHMAN'S NEW TATOU IN BEVERLY HILLS
evokes the Copacabana and night clubbing during the height of
Hollywood's Golden Age. Located in what is actually a self-contained
entertainment complex, Tatou complements an upstairs dance club and
an art gallery. ♦ Palms ring the restaurant's main dining room, a raised
stage with grand piano the centerpiece. Live jazz and blues accompany
lunch and dinner and a world-class dance floor and light show keep
patrons dancing into the wee small hours. Both Fleischmans are betting
that the success of Tatou in New York will be relived on the West Coast.
Says Mark, "Los Angelenos generally have a short attention span, so we've
done everything we can to be exciting every night." ♦ Chef Desi
Szonntagh orchestrates a three-level kitchen, bringing wit and style to a
menu that features fresh fish and grilled meats. Located in front of the
restaurant, Tatou's bistro serves lunch weekdays and is filled with
paintings by actor Tony Curtis.

**AVERAGE DINNER FOR TWO: $60**
DOES NOT INCLUDE WINE, TAX AND GRATUITY

AMERICAN
FREQUENT DINING & GIVING PROGRAM

# TRIBECA

242 NORTH BEVERLY DRIVE
BEVERLY HILLS, CA 90210
(310) 271-1595

*Visa & Major Credit Cards*
*Open Daily for Dinner • Lunch Mon-Fri*

*Proprietors*
JERRY RUBACKY
JACK DeNICOLA

*Chef*
DAVID D'AMORE

## Menu Highlights

*Appetizers*
MINIATURE MARYLAND
CRABCAKES WITH CREOLE
REMOULADE • CALIFORNIA ROLL
OF MARINATED SALMON, CUCUM-
BER & AVOCADO • SPINACH
CRÊPES WITH FOUR CHEESES &
SMOKED ROMA TOMATO SAUCE

*Entrées*
GRILLED GLAZED SALMON
WITH FRIED LEEKS & VEGETABLE
COUSCOUS • BLACKENED SHRIMP
& SEA SCALLOPS ON A BED OF
BRAISED GREENS • CRISPY DUCK
WITH CHARRED CABBAGE &
PLUM GINGER SAUCE

DRAMA, VARIETY AND ACTION ARE THE KEYS TO TRIBECA. PASSING the lively downstairs bar, guests climb a curved stairway to a spacious dining room with vaulted ceilings and liberal touches of wood, leather, marble and copper. A second upstairs bar encourages quiet conversation and is the perfect spot for a late-night bite. ♦ Executive Chef David D'Amore has created a menu of regional American classics: New England chowders and fish stews, Hawaiian fish specialties, Creole dishes and remoulades and Northwestern chutneys and relishes. Specials change daily to utilize seasonal delicacies such as soft shell crab and wild mushrooms. On every table is a bottle of extra-virgin olive oil to enjoy with baskets full of crusty bread. ♦ The project of four East Coast restaurateurs, Tribeca is now a Beverly Hills tradition, embracing the style of both Los Angeles and New York.

**AVERAGE DINNER FOR TWO: $60**
DOES NOT INCLUDE WINE, TAX AND GRATUITY

# TRADER VIC'S

THE BEVERLY HILTON
9876 WILSHIRE BLVD.
BEVERLY HILLS, CA 90210
(310)-276-6345

*Visa & Major Credit Cards*
*Open Daily • Dinner Only*

*General Manager*
GARY MURANAKA

*Executive Chef*
ELMO YEE

## Menu Highlights

*Appetizers*
COCO SHRIMP
• COSMO TIDBITS
• LUMPIA SPRING ROLLS

*Entrées*
INDONESIAN LAMB ROAST
• BARBECUED MONGOLIAN
NEW YORK STEAK
• BREAST OF DUCK
SEASONED WITH SPICES &
CHUTNEY PEACH
• COQUILLES ST. JACQUES
MOOREA: TAHITIAN-STYLE
SCALLOPS LACED WITH VELOUTE,
COCONUT, AVOCADO SAUCE

IN A TOWN KNOWN FOR CREATING FANTASY, TRADER VIC'S AT THE Beverly Hilton has been doing its share for more than thirty years. Nautical artifacts from Polynesia and Peru evoke an exotic, South Seas atmosphere that reflects the vision of the restaurant's namesake and founder, the late Victor (The Trader) Bergeron. Known as the inventor of the celebrated Mai Tai, he also introduced many other tropical rum and fruit drinks served in Trader Vic's festive lounge bar. ♦ Although the cuisine has a marked Polynesian influence, Chef Elmo Yee often combines foods and techniques from Europe, India and the Far East to create exciting new tastes. Like their ancient prototypes from the Han Dynasty, Chinese oak-burning ovens cook meat and fish dishes indirectly to retain natural juices, adding a distinctive woodsmoke flavor in the process. Among the favorite dishes are pupus, the famous finger foods that include barbecued spareribs, singed Ahi tuna, and main dishes such as Chilean sea bass with sweet ginger soy sauce.

**AVERAGE DINNER FOR TWO: $75**
DOES NOT INCLUDE WINE, TAX AND GRATUITY

To savor the magic that is Beverly Hills, begin

here.  Spend the afternoon

strolling down palm-lined boulevards, window

shopping along Rodeo Drive or soaking up the

California sun by the pool.

Indulge your senses at any one of our three

fine restaurants. Or just tell the world to go

away  and leave you all alone.

Together.

*the Beverly Hilton*

at the heart of Beverly Hills

*Call 1-800-HILTONS or your professional travel agent*

**CALIFORNIA**
FREQUENT DINING & GIVING PROGRAM

# TRYST

401 NORTH LA CIENEGA
LOS ANGELES, CA 90048
(310) 289-1600

*Visa & Major Credit Cards*
*Open Daily • Dinner Only*

Proprietor
**MARIO OLIVER**

Chef
**RALF MARHENCKE**

## Menu Highlights

*Appetizers*
CURRIED ENGLISH PEA SOUP
• PENNE & ROCK SHRIMP, LIGHT
CURRY SAUCE & SWEET PEPPERS
• DUNGENESS CRAB SALAD WITH
SLICED CUCUMBERS & LIGHT
GARLIC SAUCE

*Entrées*
CRISPY CHINESE AIRDRIED
DUCK, WILD RICE & GINGER
CHERRY SAUCE • WHOLE FRIED
CATFISH WITH FINE CUT VEGETA-
BLES & LIME-MUSTARD SAUCE

TRYST HAS BEEN A SUCCESS SINCE THE NIGHT IT OPENED ITS doors. Completely refinished by designer Ron Meyers with generous use of wood, beveled glass and fauvist paintings, the celebrity studded restaurant, located on La Cienega Boulevard's restaurant row in the middle of West Los Angeles, evokes 1940s France. And it's one of the few eateries in the city open until 2 AM. ♦ Owner of the popular nightclub, Vertigo, Mario Oliver has at Tryst discovered a formula that combines the best elements of a bistro with the convivial and intimate atmosphere of a European salon. As a result, everyone wants to get in. ♦ Native German Chef Ralf Marhencke has an eclectic palette. He serves everything from small pizza to a marvelous bouillabaisse, as well as one of the best chicken and mashed potato dishes in town. Or, as you watch the parade of luminaries who often happen by, try the prix-fixe seasonal menu. Its price is the only thing at Tryst that isn't stellar.

**AVERAGE DINNER FOR TWO: $50**
DOES NOT INCLUDE WINE, TAX AND GRATUITY

*Add some sparkle to your meals.*

## S.PELLEGRINO

*Sparkling Natural Mineral Water*
*Bottled at the Source, San Pellegrino, Italy.*
*Since 1899.*

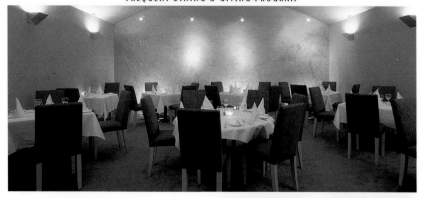

# VALENTINO

3115 PICO BOULEVARD
SANTA MONICA, CA 90405
(310) 829-4313

*Major Credit Cards*
*Closed Sunday • Dinner Only*

*Proprietor*
PIERO SELVAGGIO

*Chef*
ANGELO AURIANA

## Menu Highlights

*Appetizers*
WARM LOBSTER SALAD
• VARIETY OF SEAFOOD
IN BROTH • SHRIMP &
STRING BEANS IN
TOMATO GARLIC • LOBSTER
CANNELLONI • DUCKLING
& MUSHROOMS

*Entrées*
LOIN OF BEEF IN
BALSAMIC VINEGAR
• SLICES OF LAMB
LOIN WITH LEMON &
AROMATIC HERBS
• GRILLED SWORDFISH
WITH LEMON &
ONIONS • VEAL SHANKS

PIERO SELVAGGIO'S VALENTINO HAS HEADED THE LOS ANGELES pack of fine Italian restaurants for more than twenty years. The native Sicilian has kept his lead not by staying the same but by showing the way in food and style. A few years ago, he transformed Valentino's into a sleek showpiece for contemporary Italian cuisine. ♦ Piero has trained so many chefs who have since opened their own places that his kitchen is nick-named "Valentino's School." The lessons learned here are unforgettable: use the best ingredients, keep up with the latest in Italian cuisine, adapt to new trends, but never lose your distinctive personality. ♦ Embodying that philosophy today is Chef Angelo Auriana, a native of Bergamo. He and Piero carefully review the menu, keeping some favorites, updating others and adding new creations. Known as one of the city's greatest hosts, Piero will often suggest a menu and pair each dish with a wine from his 1,300-label collection, the largest in Los Angeles and winner of *The Wine Spectator* Grand Award since 1981.

**AVERAGE DINNER FOR TWO: $90**
DOES NOT INCLUDE WINE, TAX AND GRATUITY

# WATER GRILL

544 SOUTH GRAND AVENUE
AT SIXTH STREET
LOS ANGELES, CA 90071
(213) 891-0900

*Visa & Major Credit Cards*
*Open Daily for Dinner • Lunch Mon-Fri*

*General Manager*
PHILLIP LARIMORE

*Chef*
ALLYSON THURBER

## Menu Highlights

*Appetizers*
OYSTER PLATTER, NINE VARIETIES FROM AROUND THE WORLD • SANTA BARBARA SPOT PRAWNS • DUNGENESS CRAB BISQUE

*Entrées*
SAUTÉED YUKON RIVER SALMON WITH HAZELNUTS, MORELS & PORT • SESAME-SEARED ALBACORE WITH VEGETABLE RELISH & CHINESE FIVE-SPICE SAUCE • CHILE-CRUSTED CATFISH WITH BLACK BEAN SALSA & ANCHO POTATOES

AS ITS NAME IMPLIES, THE WATER GRILL IS MADE FOR SEAFOOD lovers. At a prime location across from Checker's Hotel, the restaurant boasts a menu that categorizes seafood selections like fine wine — by region. From Hawaiian mahi mahi and Atlantic Coast softshell crabs to Arctic char and Idaho River trout, the list is a virtual map of America's best fishing waters. Emphasis is on the Pacific Northwest. The Grill offers Washington steelhead, Oregon sable fish and Canadian King salmon brought in fresh from the Yukon River. A massive oyster collection highlights East and West Coast shellfish. ♦ Chef Allyson Thurber trained in London and New York before connecting with University Restaurant Group, a true force on the Southern California culinary scene. Her specialties work well with the more than 300 wines from the restaurant's cellar. Before you float away on a seafood river of no return, save room for the sour cream apple pie with cider caramel and apple cinnamon ice cream.

**AVERAGE DINNER FOR TWO: $60**
DOES NOT INCLUDE WINE, TAX AND GRATUITY

# XIOMARA

69 NORTH RAYMOND AVENUE
PASADENA, CA 91103
(818) 796-2520
*Visa & Major Credit Cards*
*Dinner Mon-Sat • Lunch Mon-Fri*

|  |  |
|---|---|
| *Proprietor*<br>XIOMARA ARDOLINA | *Chef*<br>PATRICK HEALY |

## Menu Highlights

*Appetizers*
CRISPY DUCK CONFIT SALAD
• SHELLFISH BOUILLABAISSE
WITH POTATO ROUILLE
• CRUNCHY MUSSEL &
RISOTTO CAKES

*Entrées*
COUNTRY CASSOULET
• CRISPY SALMON PEPPER STEAK
• LAYERED LAMB SHANK &
EGGPLANT CAKES
• SADDLE OF RABBIT
WITH SWISS CHARD

THE HISTORIC SECTION OF OLD PASADENA OFFERS SOME OF THE latest stylish dining in Southern California. In her new venture here, Xiomara Ardolina teams up with Chef Patrick Healy to explore the latest in French Country cuisine. She is the former owner of The Epicurean in La Cañada. He was the chef/owner of the famous Champagne restaurant in Los Angeles where his country fare gained a top-notch reputation. One of the dishes he's known for is a crispy salmon pepper steak with mashed potatoes made with white cheddar shavings. The Provençal lamb daube stew served at table in its own cast iron pot is another. A special treat and good value is the "Country Bistro Menu" which offers a three-course meal for only $25. If you're in the mood for dessert, try the floating island, a caramel-encrusted meringue set adrift in a sea of praline mousseline sauce or the upside-down tarte Tatin with Calvados ice cream. ♦ Xiomara's sleek, black lacquered chairs, contemporary tapestry banquettes and ceiling-high beveled mirrors dramatically contrast the restaurant's 100-year-old exposed brick wall, a notable visual focal point.

**AVERAGE DINNER FOR TWO: $55**
DOES NOT INCLUDE WINE, TAX AND GRATUITY

# YUJEAN KANG

67 NORTH RAYMOND AVENUE
AT UNION STREET
PASADENA, CA 91103
(818) 585-0855

*Major Credit Cards*
*Open Daily • Lunch & Dinner*

*Proprietor*
YVONNE KANG

*Chef/Proprietor*
YUJEAN KANG

## Menu Highlights

*Appetizers*
PACIFIC SNAPPER WITH
KUMQUAT & PASSION FRUIT
SAUCE • SUGAR PEA SPROUTS
WITH FRIED TOFU & JAPANESE
SHAVED BONITO DRESSING
• QUAIL WITH MUSHROOMS
• CHEF'S DAILY SELECTION
OF DIM SUM

*Entrées*
DUCK SMOKED IN JASMINE
TEA LEAVES • LOBSTER WITH
ASSORTED MUSHROOMS,
FAVA BEANS & CAVIAR
• VEAL WITH MATCHSTICK YAMS

ALTHOUGH CHEF/PROPRIETOR YUJEAN KANG COMES FROM A VERY traditional family of Taiwanese restaurateurs, he is recognized for a markedly untraditional approach to Chinese cuisine. Says the young chef and owner, "Our food rediscovers original Chinese dishes and transforms their classic elements and ideas into something not done before." One way that Kang accomplishes this is by counter balancing flavors in surprising ways. For instance, the sweetness of a date sauce in his lamb Hunan-style is offset by the saltiness of the prosciutto that adorns it. ♦ Yujean Kang is one of the few Asian restaurants in Southern California to offer an extensive wine list, including some rare vintages from around the world. If you've never tried it, fruit-flavored Belgian beer is a standout on the restaurant's unusual beverage menu. ♦ Right in the heart of old Pasadena, Yujean Kang's small dining room is soothingly decorated with subtle sketches of flowers and birds, hand-drawn by Kang's mother, Yufong.

**AVERAGE DINNER FOR TWO: $40**
DOES NOT INCLUDE WINE, TAX AND GRATUITY

Spago

LAS VEGAS

Cafe   Restaurant - Banquet Rooms

The Forum At Caesars - 3500 Las Vegas Boulevard South - Las Vegas, Nevada 89109

Tel: 702.369.6300

# Jacket and tie not required.

*Alamo features fine General Motors cars like this Cadillac Sedan DeVille.*

Experience the spacious luxury and smooth ride of a Cadillac Sedan DeVille from Alamo. If a Buick Regal or Pontiac Sunbird Convertible is more your style, you'll find a wide selection to choose from at all of our nationwide locations, over half of which are on-airport. And since saving money never goes out of style, the miles are always free.

For reservations, call your Professional Travel Agent or Alamo directly at **1-800-GO-ALAMO.** And savor another fine driving experience from Alamo.

**Alamo**
Rent A Car

Where all the miles are free*

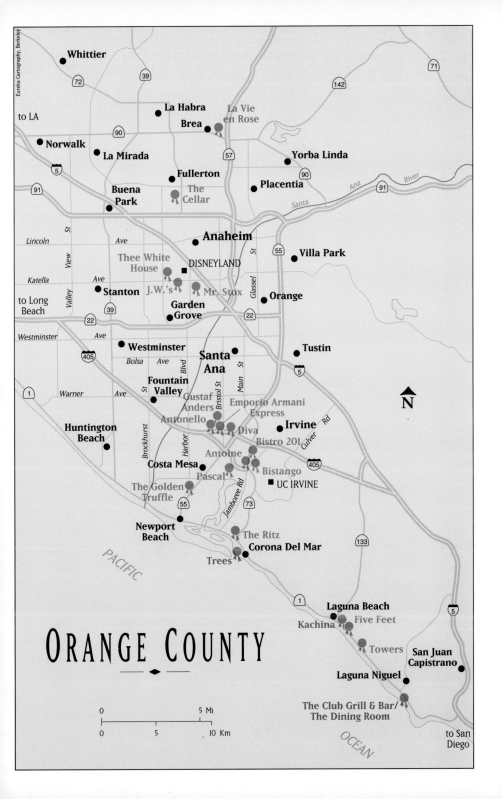

Whittier

72    39

to LA

Norwalk

La Mirada

La Habra

Brea

La Vie
en Rose

Yorba Linda

90

57

142

71

5

91

90

91      River

Santa    Ana

Buena
Park

Fullerton

The
Cellar

Placentia

Lincoln    St    Ave

View St

Katella    Ave

Ave

Anaheim

Thee White
House

DISNEYLAND

J.W.'s

Mr. Stox

Garden
Grove

Glassel St

55

Villa Park

Orange

to Long
Beach

22    39

Stanton

22

Westminster    Ave

405

Westminster

Bolsa    Ave

Santa
Ana

Main St

Tustin

5

Bristol St

Blvd

Warner    Ave

1

Fountain
Valley

Gustaf
Anders

Antonello

Emporio Armani
Express

Diva

Huntington
Beach

Brockhurst

Harbor

Antoine

Bistro 201

Pascal

Costa Mesa

Bistango

Culver Rd

Irvine

405

UC IRVINE

N

The Golden
Truffle

55

Jamboree Rd

73

Newport
Beach

The Ritz

Trees

Corona Del Mar

133

PACIFIC

1

Laguna Beach

Kachina

Five Feet

Towers

San Juan
Capistrano

ORANGE COUNTY

Laguna Niguel

The Club Grill & Bar/
The Dining Room

5

to San
Diego

OCEAN

0          5 Mi

0      5      10 Km

Eureka Cartography, Berkeley

At the Skeabost House Hotel
there are no TVs, no phones
and eight miles of the best fishing
in Scotland.
So who needs a pot of gold?
Taste the true flavor of Scotland,
Dewar's "White Label."

# ANTOINE
LE MERIDIEN HOTEL

4500 MacArthur Boulevard
Newport Beach, CA 92660
(714) 476-2001
*Visa & Major Credit Cards*
*Closed Sunday & Monday • Dinner Only*

*Maître d'/Manager*
MARCEL KOOYENGA

*Chef*
JEAN PIERRE
LEMANISSIER

## Menu Highlights

*Appetizers*
CREAM OF LENTIL WITH
FLAN OF CELERY • RAVIOLI OF
SMOKED LOBSTER WITH VIRGIN
OLIVE OIL, TOMATO & BASIL
• MILLEFEUILLE OF FRESH FOIE
GRAS WITH TRUFFLE DRESSING

*Entrées*
TOURNEDOS OF SALMON
WITH RED WINE SAUCE &
MASHED POTATOES IN OLIVE OIL
• ROASTED FILET OF SEA BASS
WITH A CRUST OF FRESH HERBS
• SAUTÉED VEAL CHOP WITH A
ZINFANDEL & MOREL SAUCE

LE MERIDIEN HOTELS ARE KNOWN FOR THEIR EXCELLENT restaurants, and Antoine more than does justice to that reputation. Designed by Lou Cataffo, the dining room is understated and elegant, with large bouquets of fresh flowers, handsome wood furnishings, original paintings and the intimate ambiance that is the hallmark of Le Meridien. ♦ Chef Jean Pierre Lemanissier has the soul of an artist. This French native's imagination and creativity touch every aspect of his cuisine, from subtle tastes and exciting textures to beautifully composed presentations. The former chef at the Four Seasons' Garden Room, he worked at Ma Maison after apprenticing with Paul Bocuse and studying in the Orient for several years. Together with consulting chef Gerard Vie, owner/chef of Les Trois Marches in Versailles, Chef Lemanissier mixes traditional French and contemporary flavors. ♦ To complement the fare, maître d'/manager Marcel Kooyenga oversees the dining room in refined style.

**AVERAGE DINNER FOR TWO: $90**
DOES NOT INCLUDE WINE, TAX AND GRATUITY

ITALIAN
FREQUENT DINING & GIVING PROGRAM

# ANTONELLO

1611 SUNFLOWER AVENUE
SANTA ANA, CA 92704
(714) 751-7153

*Visa & Major Credit Cards*
*Dinner Mon-Sat • Lunch Mon-Fri*

*General Manager*
LANA DE SALVO
*Proprietor*
ANTONIO CAGNOLO

*Chef*
CARLITO JOCSON
*Sous Chef*
FRANCO BARONE

## Menu Highlights

*Appetizers*
CARPACCIO OF BEEF
WITH PINENUTS &
OLIVES • GNOCCHI
WITH FONTINA
TOMATO SAUCE

*Entrées*
ROASTED FREE-RANGE
VEAL CHOP WITH
PORCINI & BLACK
TRUFFLES • THINLY
SLICED SWORDFISH
GRILLED WITH
FIVE-HERB SAUCE

WITH ITS GRACEFUL SHUTTERS, FRAGRANT WINDOW BOXES AND unmistakably Northern Italian cuisine, Antonello Ristorante belongs on a quaint side street in Portofino. Opened ten years ago in the spacious South Coast Plaza Village, Antonello is certainly in Southern California, but like its proprietor, Antonio Cagnolo, it is deeply rooted in Italian tradition. ♦ A childhood dream turned reality, Antonello was the product of Cagnolo's many years of training, starting with Sitmar Cruises and proceeding to the management of Alfredo's in Santa Ana's Westin Hotel. Assisted by the outstanding and innovative culinary talents of chef Carlito Jocson, Cagnolo has created a restaurant with authenticity and verve, emphasizing "Cucina Leggera," or lighter fare. ♦ Unpretentious yet gracious, the service could not be more finely orchestrated.

**AVERAGE DINNER FOR TWO: $55**
DOES NOT INCLUDE WINE, TAX AND GRATUITY

# BISTANGO

19100 VON KARMAN AVENUE
IRVINE, CA 92715
(714) 752-5222

*Visa & Major Credit Cards*
*Open Daily for Dinner • Lunch Mon-Fri*

| *Proprietor* | *Chef* |
| JOHN GHOUKASSIAN | PAUL GSTREIN |

### Menu Highlights
▼▼▼
*Appetizers*
WILD MUSHROOM SALAD
WITH ROASTED PEPPERS
• ARUGULA, GRILLED EGGPLANT,
SWEET ONION & ROASTED
TOMATOES
*Entrées*
AHI TUNA
GRILLED MEDIUM RARE
ON WARM VEGETABLE SALAD
IN SESAME SOY VINAIGRETTE

A DAZZLING EXAMPLE OF ORANGE COUNTY'S WAVE OF FINE NEW restaurants, Bistango offers visual excitement along with excellent bistro fare. Housed in Irvine's towering Atrium Building behind mountains of glass, its colorful, high-tech walls, stunning marble lounges and contemporary art displays decorate a bold, multilevel environment. ♦ Owner John Ghoukassian worked closely with architects and designers to create an uptempo mood that would take diners smoothly from day to night, from indoor to outdoor dining, from festive lunches or serious business meetings to romantic evenings for two. Nightly entertainment includes jazz and Latin sounds. ♦ The sizzle in the kitchen comes from young Austrian-born Chef Paul Gstrein. His contemporary California cuisine is unique and a welcome addition to Orange County's repertoire of fine restaurants.

**AVERAGE DINNER FOR TWO: $50**
DOES NOT INCLUDE WINE, TAX AND GRATUITY

# BISTRO 201

18201 VON KARMAN AVENUE
IRVINE, CA 92715
(714) 553-9201

*Visa & Major Credit Cards*
*Dinner Mon-Sat • Lunch Mon-Fri*

|   |   |
|---|---|
| *Proprietor* | *Chef* |
| DAVID WILHELM | THOMAS TRAN |

## Menu Highlights

*Appetizers*

SMOKED SALMON
ON POTATO CAKE WITH
SHALLOT CREAM & TWO CAVIARS
• MAINE LOBSTER CAKES
WITH CORN SALAD, ROASTED
RED PEPPERS & MUSTARD SAUCE

*Entrées*

ROASTED SEA BASS
ON POTATO PURÉE WITH
MUSTARD SAUCE & CRISPY
ONION FRITTERS • GRILLED
BREAST OF DUCK WITH LEG
CONFIT IN MICHIGAN SUNDRIED
CHERRY SAUCE • RARE AHI
PEPPER STEAK WITH
CITRUS BUTTER

SET IN BUSY KOLL CENTER, BISTRO 201 HAS A BOOMING LUNCH business. Executives meet for the restaurant's zesty interpretation of French bistro fare, and then reconvene after work for its substantial happy hour. At night, a small jazz band entertains diners, often after a performance at the nearby Orange County Performing Arts Center. The lively bar entices a local and tourist clientele late into the night. ♦ Bistro 201's friendly tone is initiated by its owner, David Wilhelm. He has imported a light bistro touch to his restaurant. Both waiters and waitresses wear white blouses with black trousers and vests in snappy bistro style, and the dishes — mostly pasta, meat and seafood plates — are wholesome and fresh. ♦ The restaurant's sparkling decor beautifully frames the cuisine. Stunning mobile light fixtures and lilac accents throughout the dining room soften the restaurant's high-tech metal chairs and sponge-painted amber walls. Windows look out on the Center's outdoor sculptures and waterfalls. Diners can enjoy the bright California sun on the patio, shaded by canvas umbrellas and surrounded by bamboo and birds of paradise.

**AVERAGE DINNER FOR TWO: $50**
DOES NOT INCLUDE WINE, TAX & GRATUITY

**FRENCH**
FREQUENT DINING & GIVING PROGRAM

# THE CELLAR

305 NORTH HARBOR BOULEVARD
FULLERTON, CA 92632
(714) 525-5682

*Visa & Major Credit Cards*
*Closed Sunday & Monday • Dinner Only*

*Maître d'*
SEAN LEWIS
*Proprietor*
ERNEST ZINGG

*Chef*
STEFAN BRUNNER

## Menu Highlights

*Appetizers*
SMOKED VENISON
WITH BUTTON MUSHROOMS
IN HAZELNUT-RASPBERRY
VINAIGRETTE
• GRILLED SEA SCALLOPS WITH
A THREE BELLPEPPER RELISH
• BAKED BRIE IN PUFF PASTRY
WITH WALNUT-PEAR SOUR CREAM

*Entrées*
SAUTÉED VEAL MEDALLIONS
WITH SUNDRIED TOMATOES
IN A BASIL CREAM SAUCE
• BRAISED SWEETBREADS
IN PORT WINE SAUCE
WITH BABY VEGETABLES

UNDER THE VILLA DEL SOL FOUR MILES NORTH OF DISNEYLAND IS what must be Southern California's most enchanting cellar: a cozy, romantic grotto created by the artistic crews of Disneyland. The restaurant's three dining areas recreate a fabulous wine cellar complete with stone walls, pillars, wine casks and ceiling beams. ♦ Originally opened in 1969, The Cellar was taken over by Ernest and Trudy Zingg in 1985. The Ziggs are the former owners of an award-winning restaurant in Canada and have been in the restaurant business for more than thirty years. ♦ Moving away from a strictly nouvelle approach, Chef Stefan Brunner prepares a lighter version of classical French cuisine. The wine list, one of six in the world to receive *The Wine Spectator* 1992 Grand Award, is a connoisseur's dream come true. It offers more than 850 selections from fifteen different countries, emphasizing California and French wines.

**AVERAGE DINNER FOR TWO: $70**
DOES NOT INCLUDE WINE, TAX AND GRATUITY

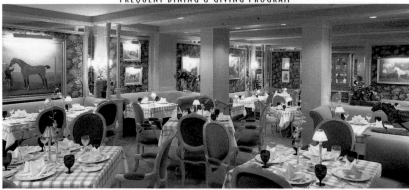

# THE CLUB GRILL & BAR

THE RITZ-CARLTON, LAGUNA NIGUEL
33533 RITZ-CARLTON DRIVE
DANA POINT, CA 92629
(714) 240-2000

*Visa & Major Credit Cards*
*Closed Tues & Wed • Dinner Only*

*Manager/Maître d'*          *Chef de Cuisine*
GRAHAM WARREN          THOMAS RUSSEL

## Menu Highlights

*Appetizers*
ESCARGOTS & WILD
MUSHROOMS IN PHYLLO, WARM
GOAT CHEESE, ROASTED PEPPERS
• SMOKED VEGETABLE RAVIOLI,
ST. ANDRE CHEESE
WITH LOBSTER ESSENCE
• CAESAR SALAD FOR TWO

*Entrées*
WOVEN BREAST OF MUSCOVY
DUCK, DRIED MICHIGAN
CHERRIES & GRAND MARNIER
• COHO SALMON NAPOLEON
WITH CRISPY POTATO LAYERS,
VINAIGRETTE OF GOLDEN
TOMATO & TARRAGON
• RACK OF NEW ZEALAND LAMB,
BLUEBERRY BOURBON SAUCE

MATCH A VIBRANT AMBIANCE WITH THE CULINARY WIT OF Chef Thomas Russel and you have The Club Grill & Bar, a restaurant that deserves its Ritz-Carlton, Laguna Niguel setting. Patterned along the lines of Annabelle's in London, The Club resembles a private jockey club, with intimate tables set amidst pictures of fox hunting and polo. Vocalists, accompanied by musical combos, lend the elegance of a 1930s-style supper club, making this a glamorous destination for both dinner and dancing. ♦ Chef Russel has triggered an enthusiastic following for his sophisticated, upbeat American cuisine. The menu features chops, steaks, seafood and homemade pasta interpreted with imagination and verve, and includes a five-course signature menu on weekends. ♦ Maître d' Graham Warren coordinates a highly skilled service staff — you'll hardly notice the deft removal of plates or timely restocking of knives. After dinner, the tempo picks up as The Club becomes a cozy rendezvous spot and late-night bar.

**AVERAGE DINNER FOR TWO: $80**
DOES NOT INCLUDE WINE, TAX AND GRATUITY

# MEDITERRANEAN
### FREQUENT DINING & GIVING PROGRAM

# THE DINING ROOM

THE RITZ-CARLTON, LAGUNA NIGUEL
33533 RITZ-CARLTON DRIVE
DANA POINT, CA 92629
(714) 240-2000
*Visa & Major Credit Cards*
*Closed Sunday & Monday • Dinner Only*

*Manager/Maître d'*
ADAM GUTTERIDGE

*Chef de Cuisine*
FABRICE CANELLE

## Menu Highlights

*Appetizers*

SHELLFISH MINESTRONE SOUP
• FRESH LOBSTER CANELLONI,
SPINACH & BLACK TRUFFLES
• WARM NEW POTATO SALAD,
DUCK CONFIT, GREEN
PEPPERCORN EMULSION

*Entrées*

ROASTED MAINE LOBSTER,
SOUFFLE OF LOBSTER CORAL &
HERB COULIS • SAUTÉED FILET
OF "DORADE," CITRUS-LEMON
THYME, NIÇOISE OLIVE RISOTTO
• COLORADO LAMB WRAPPED IN
EGGPLANT & CRISPY POTATO,
WHITE BEANS

THE ONLY SOUTHERN CALIFORNIA RESORT TO RECEIVE BOTH Mobil five-star and AAA five-diamond ratings, The Ritz-Carlton, Laguna Niguel commands an entire hilltop 150 feet above the pounding Pacific surf. Showcased amidst its grandeur is The Dining Room, an elegant testimony to fine dining. ♦ Opened nine years ago, The Dining Room is graced with the exceptional culinary talents of Chef Fabrice Canelle. Mediterranean-inspired creations such as lobster with spinach and black truffles ensure a return visit. The recipes are infused with natural jus, olive oils, fresh herbs and vegetables. ♦ The Dining Room's romantic, intimate atmosphere and friendly attitude make every guest feel welcome and comfortable. A new concept offers diners two, three, four or five courses from five categories on the menu. Prices are value-oriented and guests can mix and match menus, including special vegetarian selections.

**AVERAGE DINNER FOR TWO: $85**
DOES NOT INCLUDE WINE, TAX AND GRATUITY

# DIVA

600 ANTON STREET, SUITE 100
COSTA MESA, CA 92626
(714) 754-0600

*Visa & Major Credit Cards*
*Open Daily for Dinner • Lunch Mon–Fri*

*Manager*
SALLY VER VYNCK

*Executive Chef*
LUIS FLORES

## Menu Highlights

*Appetizers*

AHI TARTARE & WAFFLE
CHIP TORTE • SCALLOP &
WILD MUSHROOM STRUDEL
• GRILLED SHRIMP ON POTATO
PURÉE WITH MUSTARD SAUCE

*Entrées*

ULTIMATE MEAT & POTATO
DISH: FILET MIGNON SERVED
ON GRATIN POTATOES, BAKED IN
GARLIC CREAM • TWO-WAY DUCK
WITH WILD RICE POLENTA &
SOUR CHERRY SAUCE

JUST A STONE'S THROW FROM THE ORANGE COUNTY PERFORMING Arts Center and South Coast Repertory Theatre, the dramatically designed Diva caters to the theatre crowd. The restaurant allows guests to sample an eclectic California menu in classic California comfort and style. A perfect nighttime oasis, Diva is tucked in the midst of the towering office buildings near South Coast Plaza and offers dishes with names such as Killer Vegetable Plate, Ultimate Meat and Potatoes and Caviar Helper. Try the Ahi Towers, named after the office complex in which Diva is nestled, and experience slices of rare tuna presented in a towering shape of its own. ◆ Manager Sally Ver Vynck graciously oversees the lively eatery often abuzz with locals and visitors in addition to before and after-the-show diners. Tasty jazz three nights a week keeps Diva's musical inspiration alive.

**AVERAGE DINNER FOR TWO: $50**
DOES NOT INCLUDE WINE, TAX AND GRATUITY

# INTRODUCING: VIRGIN SCOTCH.

# ABERLOUR

## Virgin Scotch. Pure. Unblended. Uncompromised.

# FIVE FEET

328 GLENNEYRE STREET
LAGUNA BEACH, CA 92651
(714) 497-4955

*Visa & Major Credit Cards*
*Open Daily for Dinner • Lunch Friday Only*

|  |  |
|---|---|
| *Managers* | *Chef/Proprietor* |
| DAVID KEEFE | MICHAEL KANG |
| KYLE TWITCHELL |  |

## Menu Highlights

*Appetizers*
LIVE SOFTSHELL CRAB WITH
GREEN POPCORN BEURRE BLANC
& MANGO SALSA • CHINESE
SPICY SHRIMP RAVIOLI WITH
CILANTRO, HOT OIL & SOY
SAUCE • GOAT CHEESE WONTONS
WITH RASPBERRY SAUCE

*Entrées*
FIVE FEET'S CATFISH
WITH HOT BRAISED SAUCE
• FRESH ALASKAN HALIBUT
BAKED IN A MACADAMIA CRUST
WITH ORANGE PINEAPPLE
CINNAMON BASIL SAUCE
• HOT & SOUR CHICKEN
• VEAL CHOP ORITALIA

MICHAEL KANG NEVER THOUGHT HE'D BE THE CHEF/OWNER OF A restaurant. His restaurateur father wanted him to be a doctor, but Kang, who came to Southern California from Taiwan as a child, chose architecture over medicine. After just a few years in practice, he persuaded his sister, brother-in-law and two friends to take a chance with him on a restaurant. Now he owns two eateries, Five Feet in Laguna and Five Feet Too in Newport Beach. ♦ In an ultramodern gray-and-black setting of concrete walls, neon lights and tubular steel chairs, all centered on an open kitchen, Kang redefines Chinese food as most Americans know it. His freewheeling combinations of East and West — such as wonton filled with goat cheese or soft-shell crabs with a pineapple cilantro salsa — are served European-style on beautifully garnished plates. Kang changes the menu every six weeks and claims he fights boredom by inventing half a dozen dishes a week. ♦ What does the chef like to drink with his food? Champagne. "It goes with almost everything."

**AVERAGE DINNER FOR TWO: $50**
DOES NOT INCLUDE WINE, TAX AND GRATUITY

# EMPORIO ARMANI EXPRESS

3333 BRISTOL STREET
COSTA MESA, CA 92626
(714) 754-0300
*Visa & Major Credit Cards*
*Open Daily • Lunch & Dinner*

*General Manager*
EVAN PACE

*Chef*
ANTONIO PAGANO

## Menu Highlights

*Appetizers*
RED KIDNEY BEANS SAUTÉED WITH AHI & ONIONS IN GARLIC OLIVE SAUCE • CLAMS, MUSSELS, CALAMARI, SHRIMP & SCALLOPS MARINATED WITH TOMATOES, OLIVES & ARTICHOKES

*Entrées*
HOUSEMADE TORTELLINI FILLED WITH SEA BASS & RICOTTA, SAUTÉED IN LEMON BASIL CREAM SAUCE • ARBORIO RICE WITH BUTTON MUSHROOMS & CHOPPED CHICKEN IN SAFFRON CHICKEN STOCK

THE FIRST ARMANI RESTAURANT TO OPEN IN THE UNITED STATES, Emporio Armani Express in South Coast Plaza, has been in operation since 1991. From day one, shoppers and locals never had it so good, dropping in to dine over pizza from a wood-burning oven and pasta that is housemade. General Manager Evan Pace oversees the casual dining room with a sense of humor and style, and Chef Antonio Pagano orchestrates a menu that emphasizes a wide variety of fresh pasta, from *taliolini all'arrabiata* to *gnocchi di spinaci*. The pizza to try is the simple "Quattro Stagioni," a transeasonal medley of mushrooms, artichokes and prosciutto. Another is Pagano's "Salmone e Gamberi" with smoked salmon and prawns. ♦ The restaurant's signature dessert is tiramisu, meaning "pick me up" in Italian, and the perfect counterpoint to a long, exhausting day of shopping.

**AVERAGE DINNER FOR TWO: $40**
DOES NOT INCLUDE WINE, TAX AND GRATUITY

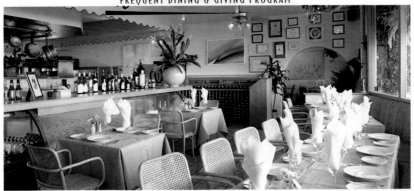

# THE GOLDEN TRUFFLE

1767 NEWPORT BOULEVARD
COSTA MESA, CA 92627
(714) 645-9858

*Major Credit Cards*
*Dinner Tues-Sat • Lunch Tues-Fri*

*Chef/Proprietor*
ALAN GREELEY

*Coordinating Chef*
LOUIS MANGINELLI

## Menu Highlights

*Appetizers*

FLORIDA STONE CRAB
SPRING ROLLS WITH WASABI

• JAMAICAN JERK
CHICKEN SALAD

• SMOKED SHRIMP &
TOMATO SALAD

*Entrées*

GYPSY CHICKEN WITH
CARIBBEAN SEASONINGS

• PRIME ANGUS RIBEYE STEAK
WITH SHIITAKE AU JUS

• ASPARAGUS RAVIOLI
WITH CILANTRO NAGE

NOW ENTERING ITS SECOND DECADE, THE UNPRETENTIOUS Golden Truffle has made its mark, thanks to Owner/chef Alan Greeley's exceptional direction. Except for inspiration, he leaves little to chance. Greeley takes ingredients that are fresh and available and works with them in his own way, making The Golden Truffle a culinary amusement park for adults, always exciting and filled with surprises. ♦ Although Greeley, named 1993 Chef of the Year by the Southern California Restaurant Writers, makes his French/Caribbean style of cooking look easy, don't be fooled. His expertise enables him to turn the familiar into novel combinations and beautiful presentations. Eye appeal and sensual textures are just as important to him as great flavors and aromas. Just tell him what you like, or order the restaurant's highly recommended prix-fixe lunch or dinner. Then sit back and enjoy one of the most memorable meals of your life.

**AVERAGE DINNER FOR TWO: $50**
DOES NOT INCLUDE WINE, TAX AND GRATUITY

**SWEDISH/CONTINENTAL**
FREQUENT DINING & GIVING PROGRAM

# GUSTAF ANDERS

SOUTH COAST PLAZA VILLAGE
AT BEAR & SUNFLOWER
SANTA ANA, CA 92704
(714) 668-1737
*Visa & Major Credit Cards*
*Open Daily • Dinner Only*

*Proprietor*
WILLIAM GUSTAF
MAGNUSON

*Chef/Proprietor*
ULF ANDERS
STRANDBERG

## Menu Highlights

*Appetizer*
COGNAC & SAGE
CURED FILET OF BEEF
SERVED THINLY SLICED, WITH
PARMESAN & TRUFFLE OIL

*Entrées*
FILET OF BEEF WITH
STILTON & RED WINE
SAUCE, CREAMED MORELS
• ROASTED THIGH &
BREAST OF DUCK OVER
BRAISED SAVOY CABBAGE
• OVEN-ROASTED RACK OF
VENISON, LINGON BERRY &
MUSHROOM SAUCE

ONE OF SOUTHERN CALIFORNIA'S MORE EXCITING EATERIES IS located across the street from Orange County's illustrious South Coast Plaza. With its tasteful, subtle decor and impeccable service, the restaurant consistently offers some of the finest Swedish, Continental and American cuisine around. Stockholm native William Gustaf Magnuson brings a smorgasbord of Nordic tastes and a generous dose of hospitality to this tiny Santa Ana nook. ◆ Recently Chef Ulf Anders Strandberg became the first from the region to prepare a meal for the world-famous James Beard Foundation. Dishes included Gustaf Anders's often requested gravlax, and wild rice pancake topped with smoked salmon, caviar and crème fraîche. The restaurant's house-baked breads and iced aquavit perfectly complement the herring or a hearty chunk of thick Vasterbotten cheese. Don't overlook the large selection of caviars.

**AVERAGE DINNER FOR TWO: $66**
DOES NOT INCLUDE WINE, TAX AND GRATUITY

**FRENCH**
FREQUENT DINING & GIVING PROGRAM

# J.W.'s
ANAHEIM MARRIOTT HOTEL

700 WEST CONVENTION WAY
ANAHEIM, CA 92802
(714) 750-0900

*Visa & Major Credit Cards*
*Open Daily • Dinner Only*

*Manager/Maître d'*
JAMES CONWAY

*Chef*
JOHN MCLAUGHLIN

## Menu Highlights

*Appetizers*
SALAD OF LOBSTER,
ARTICHOKE HEARTS, SLICED
AVOCADO & ROASTED PEPPERS
WITH HAZELNUT OIL
DRESSING • ESCARGOTS &
CRISPY SWEETBREADS IN
PUFF PASTRY

*Entrées*
SALMON FILET STEAMED
INSIDE A CRISPY POTATO
CRUST WITH THREE VEGETABLE
SAUCES • MEDALLIONS OF
WILD TEXAS BOAR
SAUTÉED WITH CALVADOS &
FRESH FETTUCCINI

A SHORT RIDE FROM DISNEYLAND AND THE ANAHEIM CONVENTION
Center, J.W.'s in the Anaheim Marriott is a good choice for those seeking
a special night out. Its high ceilings, nineteenth-century furniture and
large, wood-burning fireplace lend a baronial ambiance. Patrons dine in
intimate, subtly lit private libraries, each with its own name and decor, as
if they were guests in a private manor. ♦ Trained at New York's Culinary
Institute of America, Chef John McLaughlin presents haute cuisine that
is decidedly French, but with charming innovations expressed particularly
well with seafood and wild game. His "wine-taster" dinners are well conceived and colorfully presented. ♦ In 1985 and 1986 the Southern
California Restaurant Writers Association honored J.W.'s with its highest
award, the "Golden Scepter," and in 1986 named manager James Conway
Maître d' of the Year.

**AVERAGE DINNER FOR TWO: $80**
DOES NOT INCLUDE WINE, TAX AND GRATUITY

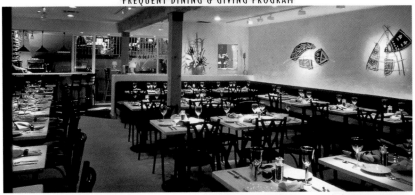

**SOUTHWESTERN**
FREQUENT DINING & GIVING PROGRAM

# KACHINA

222 FOREST AVENUE
AT PACIFIC COAST HWY.
LAGUNA BEACH, CA 92651
(714) 497-5546
*Visa & Major Credit Cards*
*Open Daily • Lunch & Dinner*

*Proprietor/Manager*
NANCY WILHELM

*Chef*
CRESCENCIO MORALES

## Menu Highlights

*Appetizers*
MESQUITE-GRILLED,
THREE-CHEESE RELLENO
WITH PAPAYA SALSA • LOBSTER
WITH SQUASH BLOSSOM, GREEN
CHILE & CORN RISOTTO • ZUNI
BLACK BEAN & CORN SOUP

*Entrées*
FILET OF SALMON GRILLED
IN CORN HUSK WITH PUMPKIN
SEED PESTO SAUCE, SALSA &
BLACK BEANS • HERB-ROASTED
BREAST OF CHICKEN ON
PARMESAN MASHED POTATOES
WITH RED PIPIAN SAUCE

KACHINA IS A TRADITIONAL HOPI INDIAN DOLL WHICH CONTAINS the dreams of those who know how to use it. Native Californian Nancy Wilhelm seems to, and has created her own dreamy eatery just off Pacific Coast Highway in Laguna Beach. Located down the steps from the sparkling ocean, the Santa Fe-inspired dining room is whimsical and fun, the closeness of the tables allowing a free flow of conversation between strangers and the hordes of local clientele. What do they all have in common? An inability to get enough of Chef Crescencio Morales's Southwestern delights. ♦ Sunday brunch is a particular favorite for those who live nearby. Generous helpings of huevos rancheros and chicken tamales in pumpkin seed sauce are just a couple of the kitchen's irresistible temptations. The chocolate bread pudding, and black and blue berry cobbler with white chocolate ice cream, aren't resisted often either.

**AVERAGE DINNER FOR TWO: $50**
DOES NOT INCLUDE WINE, TAX AND GRATUITY

**FRENCH**
FREQUENT DINING & GIVING PROGRAM

# LA VIE EN ROSE

240 SOUTH STATE COLLEGE BOULEVARD
BREA, CA 92621
(714) 529-8333

*Visa & Major Credit Cards*
*Dinner Mon-Sat • Lunch Mon-Fri*

| *Proprietor* | *Chef/Proprietor* |
| LOUIS A. LAULHERE | PASCAL GODE |

## Menu Highlights

*Appetizers*
SALMON TARTARE SERVED
WITH SMOKED SALMON
• HOT RABBIT PATÉ IN PUFFED
PASTRY • FRESH MUSSELS
STEAMED IN APPLE CIDER

*Entrées*
VEAL SWEETBREADS
WITH CITRUS & ARUGULA
• PORK LOIN, APPLES &
CALVADOS BRANDY SAUCE
• RACK OF LAMB
WITH ROSEMARY & GARLIC

A VISIT TO LA VIE EN ROSE IS LIKE A TRIP TO THE FRENCH COUN-
tryside. A charming reproduction of a Normandy farmhouse, the restaurant offers half a dozen picturesque dining rooms, as well as tapestry-
covered nooks for conversation or enjoying an aperitif. For music lovers,
there's a piano lounge with a crackling log fire. ♦ Proprietors Louis
Laulhere and Pascal Gode emigrated to America as friends, opening the
business of their dreams. Together, they have artfully revived recipes from
the farms and seaside villages of their native Gascony and Provence. The
menu, which includes Chef Gode's splendid homemade pastries, is
accompanied by a careful selection of French and California wines. ♦ A
few minutes from the heart of Orange County, La Vie en Rose is ideal for
serious eating or a celebration. Its French name means "life is rosy," and
that's how an evening here will make you feel.

**AVERAGE DINNER FOR TWO: $75**
DOES NOT INCLUDE WINE, TAX AND GRATUITY

Buxom country
star's tour bus
breaks down
in front of your
house.

Aunt Minnie
forgot to fix her
traditional
Rocky Mountain
Oyster Soup
for Thanksgiving.

The twister
didn't touch down.

Cat eats neighbor's
Chihuahua.

WILD
TURKEY®
*Rare Breed*
KENTUCKY STRAIGHT BOURBON
*Barrel Proof*
750 ML

It's rare. Sip it accordingly.

# MR. STOX

1105 EAST KATELLA AVENUE
ANAHEIM, CA 92805
(714) 634-2994

*Visa & Major Credit Cards*
*Open-Daily for Dinner • Lunch Mon-Fri*

*Proprietors*
RON MARSHALL
CHICK MARSHALL

*Proprietor*
DEBBIE MARSHALL
*Chef*
SCOTT RACZEK

## Menu Highlights

*Appetizers*
FILET OF SMOKED SALMON
WITH PARSLEY MAYONNAISE
• CARPACCIO
• BLACK BEAN SOUP

*Entrées*
MESQUITE-GRILLED
RACK OF LAMB ON EGGPLANT,
ROSEMARY GARLIC SAUCE
• BRAISED RABBIT IN BRANDY-
PEPPERCORN SAUCE WITH
PRUNES & LEEKS
• PAN-SEARED AHI &
ORANGE GINGER SAUCE

PEOPLE DON'T GO TO ANAHEIM JUST FOR DISNEYLAND, CONVENtions and ball games. They also go to dine at Mr. Stox. The awardwinning restaurant is filled with romantic booths, Persian carpets and colorful floral arrangements that comprise several dining rooms, each with a different atmosphere. ♦ More than a restaurant, Mr. Stox represents three generations of the Marshall family's dedication to fine dining in a relaxed California environment. ♦ Excellent service and the up-todate Continental cooking of Chef Scott Raczek make that goal easily attainable. Anticipating the public's demand for freshness, Mr. Stox has its own herb garden and makes all pastries, breads and pasta in-house. Chef Raczek favors quick cooking, reduction sauces and colorful presentations, which reveal the hand-picked quality of the produce, seafood and meat he obtains. ♦ Recipient of *The Wine Spectator* Grand Award, Mr. Stox presents wine tastings and special dinners to showcase its 20,000-bottle collection of wines that come from a dozen countries and ten states.

**AVERAGE DINNER FOR TWO: $60**
DOES NOT INCLUDE WINE, TAX AND GRATUITY

# PASCAL

1000 BRISTOL STREET
AT JAMBOREE BLVD.
NEWPORT BEACH, CA 92660
(714) 752-0107

*Visa & Major Credit Cards*
*Dinner Mon-Sat • Lunch Mon-Fri*

| *Proprietor* | *Chef/Proprietor* |
| MIMI OLHATS | PASCAL OLHATS |

## Menu Highlights

*Appetizers*

LASAGNA POTATO & ESCARGOTS
• BELGIAN ENDIVE SALAD WITH
ROQUEFORT & PINENUTS
• SAUTÉED WILD MUSHROOMS
• CHEESE RAVIOLES &
DUCK CONFIT SOUP

*Entrées*

CHILEAN SEABASS WITH THYME
• SAUTÉED SWEETBREADS
WITH SHALLOTS CONFIT
• RABBIT À LA MOUTARDE
• GRILLED RACK OF BABY LAMB,
POLENTA & CASSIS SAUCE

CONSISTENTLY RATED ONE OF THE BEST RESTAURANTS IN ORANGE County, Pascal should be on the itinerary of anyone who visits the area. In a decidedly American landscape, Owners Mimi and Pascal Olhats have recreated an unexpected slice of the French countryside. With the couple's warm greetings at the door and fresh-cut flowers lovingly arranged, the restaurant exudes Gallic charm. ♦ Born in Normandy and trained in the kitchen of the legendary Paul Bocuse in Lyon, Chef/proprietor Pascal Olhats perfected his skills in St. Tropez and Le Meridien Newport Beach before opening his own restaurant. Don't let the mall location fool you. Once you enter, Pascal's authentic looking country cottage exterior appears reassuringly. ♦ Traditional Country French dishes and devotion to excellence are Olhats's specialties. Whether you're savoring a lamb salad with apple walnut dressing or succulent sea bass with thyme, it's easy to let each morsel take you to the farmlands of Normandy or the Côte d'Azur. Fittingly, when customers ask if there is a view, Pascal says with a wink, "Our view is on the plate."

**AVERAGE DINNER FOR TWO: $60**
DOES NOT INCLUDE WINE, TAX AND GRATUITY

# THE RITZ

880 NEWPORT CENTER
NEWPORT BEACH, CA 92660
(714) 720-1800

*Visa & Major Credit Cards*
*Closed Sunday • Lunch & Dinner*

| Proprietors | Executive Chef |
|---|---|
| HANS & CHARLENE | GUADALUPE CAMARENA |
| PRAGER | *Food & Beverage Director* |
| | CLAUDE KOËBERLÉ |

## Menu Highlights

*Appetizers -*
LOBSTER BISQUE • WILD
MUSHROOM CAPPUCCINO!
• DUNGENESS CRABCAKES
• STEAMED MUSSELS MARINIERE!
• THOSE RITZ EGGS
WITH CAVIAR

*Entrées*
SPIT-ROASTED RACK OF LAMB
• BOUILLABAISSE • STEAK DIANE
• DOVER SOLE MEUNIERE
• ROASTED TURBOT WITH
CHANTERELLES

IF YOU'RE IN THE MOOD FOR CONTINENTAL DINING IN A sophisticated atmosphere, try The Ritz. One of Newport Beach's most lavish restaurants, The Ritz boasts five exquisite dining rooms, solid oak paneling and a blend of warm peach and gold tones. ♦ The Ritz is owned and operated by veteran chef and restaurateur Hans Prager, whose forty-five year career has taken him from chef at Scandia to executive chef of Lawry's to founder of The Ritz in 1977. Wife Charlene and daughter Karen oversee service that caters to diners as if they were family home for a traditional holiday feast. ♦ Robust dishes such as spit-roasted lamb, bouillabaisse and Bavarian roasted duck with red cabbage and spaetzle are favorites. Daily market available fresh fish dishes are prepared in the most appropriate manner.

**AVERAGE DINNER FOR TWO: $75**
DOES NOT INCLUDE WINE, TAX AND GRATUITY

# THEE WHITE HOUSE

887 SOUTH ANAHEIM BOULEVARD
ANAHEIM, CA 92805
(714) 772-1381

*Visa & Major Credit Cards*
*Open Daily for Dinner • Lunch Mon-Fri*

Proprietor
BRUNO SERATO

Chef
PHILLIP CLARK

## Menu Highlights

*Appetizers*
CARPACCIO OF TUNA WITH
LEMON & EXTRA VIRGIN
OLIVE OIL • GNOCCHI WITH
GORGONZOLA SAUCE
• RIGATONI WITH BACON,
EGGS & PARMESAN

*Entrées*
SAUTÉED VEAL SCALLOPPINE
WITH ARTICHOKE HEARTS,
DEMI-GLACE • GRILLED
SWORDFISH WITH CITRUS
BEURRE BLANC • OVEN-
ROASTED RACK OF DOMESTIC
LAMB, HERB SAUCE

WITHIN JOGGING DISTANCE OF THE CONVENTION CENTER AND Disneyland, Thee White House is an eighty-year-old mansion restored as one of Orange County's brightest new restaurants. In a tableau of private, candlelit rooms, diners are transported to a more graceful age, where crackling log fires and elegant Victorian decor set the stage for romantic dining. ♦ Bruno Serato is a Parisian-born Italian who grew up in Verona and was trained in the old European tradition. He acquired Thee White House after refining his talents at La Vie en Rose, where he was named 1985's Maître d' of the Year by the Southern California Restaurant Writers Association. Inspired by such masters as Italy's renowned Gualtiero Marchesi, Serato and Chef Phillip Clark interpret Italian standards with a Gallic touch. Serato returns to Europe frequently to keep abreast of the latest trends in cuisine.

### AVERAGE DINNER FOR TWO: $60
DOES NOT INCLUDE WINE, TAX AND GRATUITY

# TOWERS
SURF AND SAND HOTEL

1555 SOUTH COAST HIGHWAY
LAGUNA BEACH, CA 92651
(714) 497-4477

*Visa & Major Credit Cards*
*Open Daily • Dinner Only*

*Director of Restaurants*
SAEED PESSIAN

*Chef*
PATRICK SMITH

## Menu Highlights

*Appetizers*
NAPOLEON OF SCALLOPS
WITH BRAISED RADICCHIO &
BAROLO WINE SAUCE
• SWEETBREADS STRUDEL
WITH WILD MUSHROOM,
SPINACH & LOBSTER SAUCE
• WILD RICE & CORN BLINIS
WITH OSSETRA CAVIAR

*Entrées*
TOURNEDOS OF VEAL
WITH MOREL SAUCE & POTATO
RISOTTO • GRILLED SWORDFISH
WITH LENTILS & BALSAMIC
VINEGAR SAUCE • HONEY-
CILANTRO DUCK WITH
STIR-FRIED VEGETABLES

NINE STORIES ABOVE THE POUNDING SURF, IN THE RENOVATED Surf and Sand Hotel, Towers has a magnificent view of the Pacific. Under the direction of Food and Beverage Director Gregg Desher, it has also become a first-rate restaurant serving contemporary French and Northern Italian cuisine. ♦ From the mirrored dining room that reflects the blue-green sea below to the Fireside Lounge with its baby grand piano and granite fireplace, Towers proclaims elegance and romance. Plate-glass doors etched with Art Deco designs give way to a 1930s-style dining room brightened by white Limoges china and fine crystal stemware. There, director of restaurants Saeed Pessian greets guests with warmth and graciousness, and tuxedo-clad waiters glide silently by with the sumptuous dishes of Chef Patrick Smith. ♦ An outstanding wine list adds the final touch to this sparkling restaurant surrounded by the beauty of Laguna Beach.

**AVERAGE DINNER FOR TWO: $70**
DOES NOT INCLUDE WINE, TAX AND GRATUITY

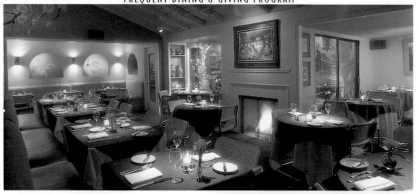

# TREES

440 HELIOTROPE
NEAR PACIFIC COAST HIGHWAY
CORONA DEL MAR, CA 92625
(714) 673-0910

*Visa & Major Credit Cards*
*Open Daily • Dinner Only*

*Proprietors*
ABBEY & RUSSELL
ARMSTRONG

*Chef*
HARRY MASON

## Menu Highlights

*Appetizers*
ASSORTED SPRING ROLLS
• WILD GREENS SALAD WITH
GLAZED WALNUTS &
GORGONZOLA • HOUSE-
SMOKED IDAHO TROUT WITH
MUSTARD MAYONNAISE

*Entrées*
BAKED MEATLOAF WITH
HOUSEMADE MASHED
POTATOES • MARYLAND-STYLE
CRABCAKES WITH MUSTARD
SAUCE • TERIYAKI GRILLED
MAHI-MAHI

AT TREES, CORONA DEL MAR'S MOST CHARMING HIDEAWAY, THE personal touch is always the special of the day. Proprietors and hosts Abbey and Russell Armstrong have put their warmth and welcome into every detail, and it shows. The soft peach walls of the three dining rooms are covered with art, and glass windows wrap around a ficus tree-filled courtyard. Fireplaces and friendly service invite a leisurely dinner. ♦ Chef/proprietor Armstrong offers an eclectic, contemporary American bistro menu with an international flavor, including a large selection of Indochine dishes. Before coming to Corona del Mar, he owned the popular Chez Russell in Sun Valley, Idaho. His varied menu of seasonal specialties has won him a loyal clientele. ♦ To prolong the pleasure of an evening at Trees, join the locals in the lounge/bar for a cappuccino by the fireplace where a piano player entertains daily. Night owls can order a light meal from the bar menu until midnight.

**AVERAGE DINNER FOR TWO: $40**
DOES NOT INCLUDE WINE, TAX AND GRATUITY

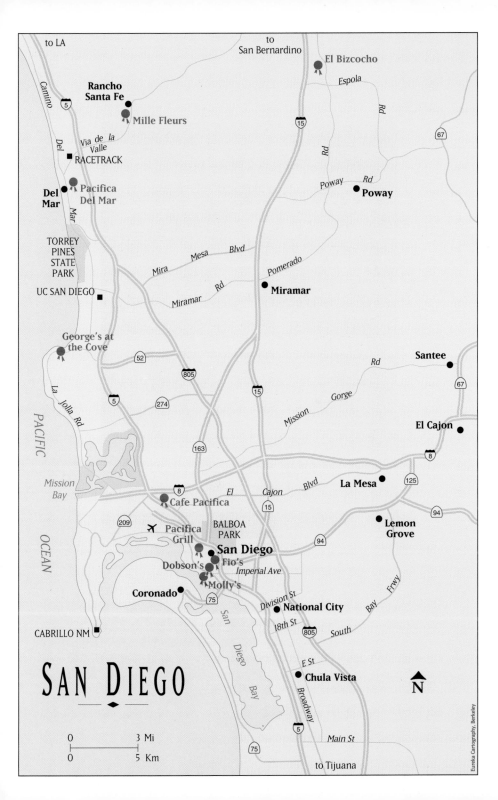

to LA

to
San Bernardino

El Bizcocho

Espola

**Rancho
Santa Fe**

5

Mille Fleurs

15

Rd

67

Via de la
Valle

■ RACETRACK

Poway Rd

**Poway**

**Del
Mar**

Pacifica
Del Mar

TORREY
PINES
STATE
PARK

Mira Mesa Blvd

Pomerado

UC SAN DIEGO ■

Miramar Rd

Miramar

**Miramar**

George's at
the Cove

52

Rd

**Santee**

805

67

5

274

15

Mission Gorge

**El Cajon**

PACIFIC

163

8

La Jolla Rd

**La Mesa**

125

Mission
Bay

8

El Cajon Blvd

94

209

15

Cafe Pacifica

94

**Lemon
Grove**

OCEAN

✈ Pacifica
Grill

BALBOA
PARK

**San Diego**

Dobson's

Fio's

Imperial Ave

Molly's

**Coronado**

75

Division St

**National City**

CABRILLO NM ■

18th St

805

South Bay Frwy

# SAN DIEGO
◆

75

E St

**Chula Vista**

N

Broadway

5

Main St

5

0        3 Mi

0        5 Km

75

to Tijuana

Eureka Cartography, Berkeley

$3,000

# This is a work of art inside a work of art.

Here you see Glenfiddich® Pure Malt Scotch Whisky exactly where it belongs. In a beautifully hand-cut crystal decanter (lead-free) with a solid sterling silver stag's head.

The stag's head recalls that Glenfiddich in Gaelic means 'Valley of the Deer.' The hand-cut crystal reveals the exceptionally smooth, rare character of 30 year-old Glenfiddich. The only Scotch that's a work of art all by itself.

*To obtain the Glenfiddich Stag's Head decanter ask your local spirits merchant or call William Grant & Sons collect at 908-225-9000.*

G L E N F I D D I C H®   P U R E   M A L T   S C O T C H   W H I S K Y

**SEAFOOD**
FREQUENT DINING & GIVING PROGRAM

# CAFE PACIFICA

2414 SAN DIEGO AVENUE
SAN DIEGO, CA 92110
(619) 291-6666

*Visa & Major Credit Cards*
*Open Daily for Dinner • Lunch Mon-Fri*

| *Proprietors* | *Chef* |
|---|---|
| DEACON BROWN | ERIC WADLUND |
| KIPP DOWNING | |

## Menu Highlights

*Appetizers*
SALMON & SWEET CORN CAKES
WITH HERB BUTTER SAUCE &
SALMON CAVIAR
• GRILLED SEA SCALLOPS, WARM
SPINACH WITH CITRUS POPPY
SEED VINAIGRETTE

*Entrées*
SPICY GARLIC SEAFOOD
FETTUCCINE • AHI
WITH SHIITAKE MUSHROOMS &
GINGER BUTTER

ONE OF THE GREAT SEAFOOD RESTAURANTS IN OLD SAN DIEGO, Cafe Pacifica was opened by Deacon Brown and Kipp Downing in August 1980, and has evolved into one of the most popular restaurants along the Southern California coast. Cafe Pacifica has won the hearts and palates of a loyal clientele who sometimes come to dine as many as three or four times a week. ♦ With Chef Eric Wadlund coordinating the cuisine, Cafe Pacifica has fine-tuned its style. His wizardry with fish hooks many a steak-and-chops fan. ♦ The comfortable dining room is understated yet fashionable, and the back patio with a screened roof makes a nice setting for lunch *al fresco*. In the evening, Cafe Pacifica is subdued and romantic; a place for quiet conversation over a bottle of wine. It's a delightful destination for fine dining in Old Town San Diego.

**AVERAGE DINNER FOR TWO: $50**
DOES NOT INCLUDE WINE, TAX AND GRATUITY

133

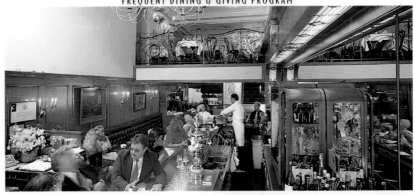

# DOBSON'S

956 BROADWAY CIRCLE
SAN DIEGO, CA 92101
(619) 231-6771

*Visa & Major Credit Cards*
*Closed Sunday • Lunch & Dinner*

*Proprietor*
**PAUL DOBSON**

*Chef*
**DEBORAH SCHNEIDER**

## Menu Highlights

*Appetizers*

MUSSEL BISQUE EN CROUTE
• ALASKAN KING CRAB,
FRESH ARTICHOKE &
HEART OF PALM SALAD
• HOT OYSTERS, BEURRE
BLANC & CAVIAR

*Entrées*

FRESH FILET OF
HOLLAND DOVER SOLE
MEUNIÈRE • FRESH BREAST
OF DUCK SAUTÉED WITH
SWEET & TART GRIOTTES,
SHERRY SAUCE • FRESH
DOMESTIC RACK OF LAMB
ROASTED WITH A RED
BURGUNDY SAUCE

ONE OF AMERICA'S FIRST MATADORS, PAUL DOBSON IS A MAN who literally fought his way to the top. His passion for bullfighting won him the respect of top political figures and the social elite both in Mexico and the United States. ♦ Dobson's decision to settle down and open an upscale restaurant in San Diego's undesirable downtown area raised more than a few eyebrows at the time. He obviously knew what he was doing; his restaurant has been booked solid since its opening, and the formerly rundown neighborhood surrounding it has undergone a dramatic revitalization crowned by the Horton Plaza shopping center. ♦ Dobson refers to his establishment as "a gentleman's bar," heavily patronized by local businessmen and attorneys. In the upstairs dining room, Chef Deborah Schneider reigns supreme, creating traditional grill fare with a Southern French flourish. The combination of low-key atmosphere and first-rate cuisine has gained Dobson's a well-deserved place in the limelight.

**AVERAGE DINNER FOR TWO: $65**
DOES NOT INCLUDE WINE, TAX AND GRATUITY

# EL BIZCOCHO

RANCHO BERNARDO INN
17550 BERNARDO OAKS DRIVE
SAN DIEGO, CA 92128
(619) 487-1611
*Visa & Major Credit Cards*
*Open Daily • Dinner Only*

| *Maître d'* | *Chef* |
|---|---|
| DAVID TOWNSEND | THOMAS B. DOWLING |

## Menu Highlights

*Appetizers*
GRILLED SCALLOPS WITH
CABBAGE & JUNIPER
BERRIES • LARGE PRAWNS
WITH FRESH TOMATO &
BEURRE BLANC

*Entrées*
ROASTED SALMON WITH
MUSTARD CRUST, BELGIAN
ENDIVE & SPINACH • SAUTÉED
VEAL CHOP WITH MOREL
CREAM SAUCE • ROASTED
DUCKLING, CARVED
TABLESIDE, SERVED WITH
APPLES & CALVADOS
BIGARADE SAUCE

THIRTY MILES FROM SAN DIEGO IN THE SAN PASQUAL MOUNTAINS, Rancho Bernardo Inn boasts two championship golf courses, twelve tennis courts, two swimming pools and a first-class French restaurant that demands to be shared with the public. El Bizcocho's mission-style dining room offers a total dining experience. Every aspect of fine dining is treated with equal importance, from the exquisite food and outstanding service to an impeccable wine list and an extensive selection of rare Cognacs and liqueurs. ♦ The restaurant's success begins with Chef Tom Dowling, a young East Coast native who graduated from the Culinary Institute of America and spent five years at the Helmsley Palace Hotel in New York City. His cuisine balances French recipes with the lighter cooking style of Southern California. ♦ El Bizcocho's excellence is confirmed by a wine list so superior it was honored with *The Wine Spectator* Award of Excellence.

**AVERAGE DINNER FOR TWO: $80**
DOES NOT INCLUDE WINE, TAX AND GRATUITY

# FIO'S

801 FIFTH AVENUE
SAN DIEGO, CA 92101
(619) 234-3467

*Visa & Major Credit Cards*
*Open Daily for Dinner • Lunch Mon–Fri*

*Proprietor*
MIKE MCGEATH

*Executive Chef*
JOSEPH SAVINO

## Menu Highlights

*Appetizers*

FRIED ARTICHOKE HEARTS
WITH PROSCIUTTO,
CHEESE & MUSHROOMS

• PIZZA WITH FENNEL SAUSAGE,
SMOKED MOZZARELLA,
BROCCOLI & SUNDRIED TOMATOES

*Entrées*

SEMOLINA PASTA SHELLS TOSSED
WITH FENNEL SAUSAGE, BROC-
COLI, RICOTTA & HOT PEPPERS

• SKEWERED BREADED VEAL
ROLLS FILLED WITH PROSCIUT-
TO, SUNDRIED TOMATOES &
ITALIAN CHEESES, WITH
SAGE-MARSALA SAUCE

*SAN DIEGO MAGAZINE'S* RESTAURANT CRITICS AND READERS POLL recently named Fio's Best Italian Restaurant for the third year in a row — an impressive achievement for a restaurant open only since December of 1989. Part of the renaissance of the Gaslamp Quarter in downtown San Diego, Fio's is a bright star in a neighborhood blooming with new restaurants, bars and boutiques. ♦ The restaurant's theme is the 800-year-old Palio horserace of Siena, and vivid murals of banner-waving participants in period costume adorn the walls. An open kitchen and lots of streetfront windows provide further visual stimulation. ♦ Executive Chef Joseph Savino, a graduate of La Varenne in Paris, France, draws upon his Italian heritage and travels throughout Europe for his menu inspiration. "We've taken the most rustic and robust dishes from Italy," says Savino, "and brought them to our kitchen with simplicity, yet style." The results are superb, especially when accompanied by one of Fio's moderately priced Italian or California wines.

**AVERAGE DINNER FOR TWO: $50**
DOES NOT INCLUDE WINE, TAX AND GRATUITY

# GEORGE'S AT THE COVE

1250 PROSPECT STREET
LA JOLLA, CA 92037
(619) 454-4244
*Visa & Major Credit Cards*
*Open Daily • Lunch & Dinner*
*Weekend Breakfast*

*Proprietor*
GEORGE HAUER

*Chef*
SCOTT MESKAN

## Menu Highlights

*Appetizers*

SALMON & SHRIMP
SAUSAGE WITH SWEET &
SOUR CABBAGE • CHARBROILED
BOB WHITE QUAIL
STUFFED WITH
WILD MUSHROOMS

*Entrées*

NEW ZEALAND LAMB
RACK CHARBROILED
WITH A GARLIC
MUSTARD DEMI-GLACE
• AHI FLASH GRILLED RARE
WITH WASABI &
POPPYSEED SAUCE

THE LA JOLLA COASTLINE IS THE HOME OF GEORGE'S AT THE COVE, a fashionable eatery run by owner George Hauer. George's affords spectacular views of the famous cove and North County beaches from all of its three levels. ♦ Downstairs, the casually elegant dining room features a menu emphasizing fresh seasonal seafood and produce prepared with a California flair. The top two levels, George's Cafe and Ocean Terrace, offer the best in casual patio dining including rotisserie chicken, pork, pastas, salads and sandwiches. ♦ Chef/proprietor Scott Meskan, a native of Georgia and one of the youngest certified chefs from that region, acquired his classical European training in Atlanta's best restaurants. His dishes feature seafood caught by local fishermen or flown in from Hawaii or Maine. The dining experience is enhanced by the sparkling ocean view and an award-winning California wine list.

**AVERAGE DINNER FOR TWO: $65**
DOES NOT INCLUDE WINE, TAX AND GRATUITY

FRENCH
FREQUENT DINING & GIVING PROGRAM

# MILLE FLEURS

6009 PASEO DELICIAS
RANCHO SANTA FE, CA 92067
(619) 756-3085

*Visa & Major Credit Cards*
*Open Daily for Dinner • Lunch Mon-Fri*

*Proprietor*
BERTRAND

*Chef*
MARTIN WOESLE

## Menu Highlights

*Appetizers*
WILD RICE GALETTE
WITH CHIVES, CREME FRAICHE
& BELUGA CAVIAR • SALAD OF
MAINE LOBSTER WITH
FRESH FENNEL & ORANGE
GINGER VINAIGRETTE

*Entrées*
OVEN-ROASTED SUMMERFIELD
FARM BABY LAMB WITH
GARLIC CONFIT & ROSEMARY
POTATO CAKE • FRESH
SEA BASS, BROILED UNDER
A BLACK OLIVE CRUST
WITH TOMATOES &
PERNOD SAUCE

IN A 1929 RANCHO SANTA FE ADOBE, FRENCHMAN BERTRAND Hug's Mille Fleurs blooms with fresh surprises. A mile down the road is the Chino family farm, where Chef Martin Woesle heads at dawn every day to select the choicest fruits and vegetables available in California. He builds his daily changing menu around what he discovers, and decorates his dishes with perhaps not a thousand but at least a dozen edible flowers. ♦ Trained in West Germany where he worked at the three-star Aubergine in Munich, Chef Woesle infuses his superb dishes with fresh herb flavors and sauces them subtly. The salads and vegetables are outstanding, as are the fruit sorbets and tarts. ♦ Exuberant and personable, Bertrand is the kind of host who remembers everyone's name. Mille Fleurs is just as charming, with whitewashed walls, exposed beams and a two-sided fireplace. There's a beautiful tiled courtyard for outdoor lunches and an intimate bar/lounge that's open well past midnight.

**AVERAGE DINNER FOR TWO: $70**
DOES NOT INCLUDE WINE, TAX AND GRATUITY

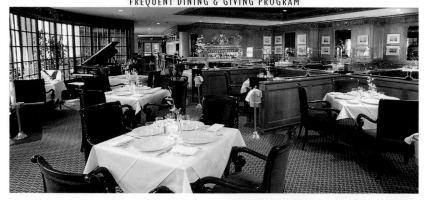

# MOLLY'S

SAN DIEGO MARRIOTT
333 WEST HARBOR DRIVE
SAN DIEGO, CA 92101
(619) 230-8909

*Visa & Major Credit Cards*
*Open Daily • Dinner Only*

*Manager & Maître d'*
NABIL BADER

*Executive Chef*
CLEMENTE LEON

## Menu Highlights

♦

*Appetizers*
CLASSIC CAESAR SALAD
• SEAFOOD WITH ARTICHOKE
HEARTS, LOBSTER, SCALLOPS,
CRAB & TARRAGON LEMON
DRESSING • SAUTÉ OF CRAB &
ASPARAGUS IN PUFFED PASTRY
WITH CREAM OF CURRY

*Entrées*
FILET MIGNON WITH CALVADOS
BRANDY SAUCE & MORELS
• ROASTED NAPA VALLEY CHICK-
EN WITH SHIITAKES, BLACK &
WHITE BEANS, SWEET PEPPERS
• RACK OF LAMB CARVED
TABLESIDE

LOCATED ON THE LOWER LEVEL OF THE SAN DIEGO MARRIOTT'S gleeming North Tower overlooking the picturesque Marina, Molly's is the epitome of elegance and romance. Outside the entrance, graceful waterfalls and a fish pond stocked with colorful and exotic finned creatures set the mood before you even walk in. ♦ Traditional tableside service is alive and well here. Maître d' Nabil Bader oversees the elaborate preparation and showmanship that make this kind of presentation unique and memorable. Mouthwatering filet mignon is cut and displayed before your eyes on a bed of scallions and sweet onions, each bite containing an explosion of flavor. Likewise the Mexican Ahi with fresh salsa, another of Chef Clemente Leon's savory signature dishes. ♦ Master Pastry Chef Rudi Weider, an eleven-year Marriott veteran, is an expert in his field. The ultimate tableside experience at Molly's is watching the preparation of Bananas Foster in true, New Orleans fashion, all drama and flaming glory.

### AVERAGE DINNER FOR TWO: $60
DOES NOT INCLUDE WINE, TAX AND GRATUITY

# PACIFICA DEL MAR

1555 Camino del Mar
Del Mar, Ca 92014
(619) 792-0476

*Visa & Major Credit Cards*
*Open Daily • Lunch & Dinner*
*• Weekend Breakfast*

*Proprietors*
KIPP DOWNING
DEACON BROWN

*Executive Chef*
JACKY SLOANE-
DONALDSON

## Menu Highlights

*Appetizers*
SMOKED CORN CHOWDER
WITH BLACK BEANS & CHICKEN
• ORIENTAL ROCK SHRIMP
STIR-FRY GARNISHED WITH
SCALLOPS • WOK-SEARED DUCK
SALAD WITH CRISP GINGER &
ENOKI MUSHROOMS

*Entrées*
SASHIMI AHI TEMPURA
WITH ASPARAGUS & WASABI
• BEEF TOURNADO WITH SHRIMP
POTATO PANCAKE & GARLIC
DEMI-GLACE • BLACKENED
SEABASS WITH AVOCADO,
CUCUMBER & TOMATO SALSA

PACIFICA DEL MAR SPORTS A DINING ROOM WITH RICH WOOD-work and distressed copper walls, giving way to a glassed-in, heated patio with a spectacular ocean view — a treat in itself. ◆ Pacifica Del Mar creates "coastal cuisine," a style of cooking that emphasizes fresh seafood and produce. Lovers of the ocean's bounty will not be disappointed by the kitchen's abundant selections. In addition, Chef Jacky Sloane-Donaldson's eclectic menu features creative pastas, salads and housemade specialty desserts to round out the Southern California dining experience. The newly refurbished bar offers the state's finest wines and is always bustling. ◆ Visitors to the nearby La Costa Spa and local residents have come to appreciate the healthy, exciting dishes and hard-to-find wines offered at Pacifica Del Mar.

### AVERAGE DINNER FOR TWO: $60
DOES NOT INCLUDE WINE, TAX AND GRATUITY

AMERICAN
FREQUENT DINING & GIVING PROGRAM

# PACIFICA GRILL & ROTISSERIE

1202 KETTNER
SAN DIEGO, CA 92101
(619) 696-9226

*Visa & Major Credit Cards*
*Open Daily for Dinner • Lunch Mon-Fri*

*Proprietors*
DEACON BROWN
KIPP DOWNING

*Chefs*
PAUL WALKER
TIMOTHY MAVRAKOS

## Menu Highlights

*Appetizers*
SHRIMP & CHICKEN DUMPLINGS
WITH SWEET CORN CREAM
• CHILE-CRUSTED LAMB RIBLETS
WITH BURNT ORANGE DIP
• MARYLAND CRABCAKES
WITH SPICY AIOLI

*Entrées*
BLUE CHEESE RAVIOLI WITH
CHICKEN & TOASTED ALMOND
PESTO • ROTISSERIE DUCK WITH
HONEY & ORANGE GLAZE
• YUCATAN BARBECUED KING
SALMON WITH FRESH LIME
• GRILLED RIBEYE WITH
SHIITAKE DEMI-GLAZE

THERE'S NOTHING ORDINARY ABOUT PACIFICA GRILL & ROTIS-
serie. The newly renovated restaurant now features a rotisserie that slowly roasts chicken, lamb and duck to succulent perfection. The same care
goes into all other dishes as well. Best described as regional American,
Pacifica's cuisine offers unusual interpretations of California dishes with
an emphasis on grilled seafood, pasta, pizza and, of course, rotisserie
poultry and meats. The restaurant's abundance of "small plates" allows
guests to wander through the menu sampling various styles of cooking.
All menu items are geared to provide not only diversity, but the freshest
products available. ♦ Celebrating its tenth year, Pacifica Grill is one of
San Diego's favorite destinations for business lunches. At night, the contemporary dining room, with its distinctive bar takes on a soft, subdued
and sophisticated downtown look.

**AVERAGE DINNER FOR TWO: $50**
DOES NOT INCLUDE WINE, TAX AND GRATUITY

YVESSAINTLAURENT

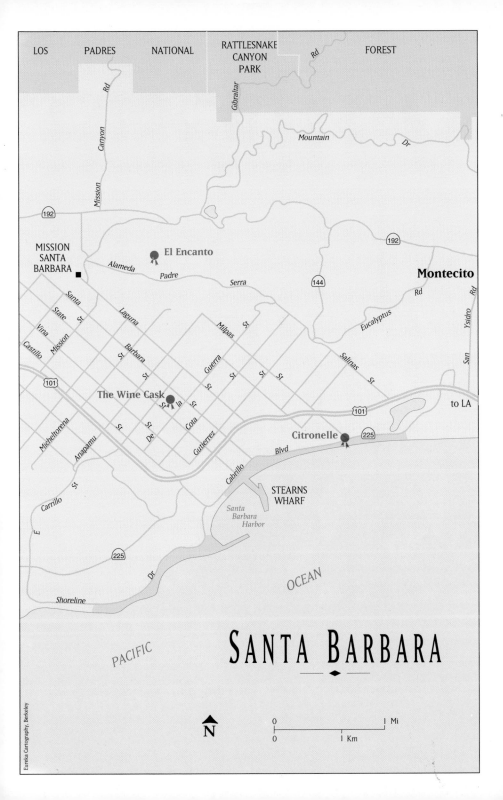

LOS    PADRES    NATIONAL    RATTLESNAKE    FOREST
CANYON
PARK

Rd

Gibraltar

Mountain    Dr

Canyon    Rd

Mission

192

MISSION
SANTA
BARBARA

El Encanto

Alameda

Padre

Serra

192

Montecito

144

Rd

Santa

State    St.

Laguna

Milpas    St.

Eucalyptus

San  Ysidro  Rd

Vina

Mission

Barbara    St.

Guerra    St.    St.    St.

Salinas    St.

Castillo

101

The Wine Cask

Sta    la    St.

Cota

De    St.

Citronelle

101

225

to LA

Micheltorena

Anapamu

St.

Gutierrez

Blvd

Cabrillo

STEARNS
WHARF

Carrillo

St.

Santa
Barbara
Harbor

E

225

OCEAN

Dr

Shoreline

PACIFIC

# SANTA BARBARA

◆

N

| 0 | | 1 Mi |
| 0 | 1 Km | |

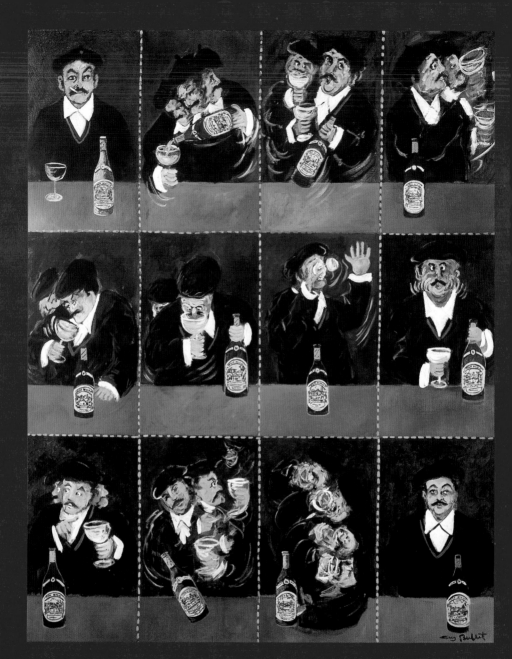

Far Niente

The Napa Valley Wine Estate

"The Art of Persuasion"

Limited Edition Lithographs of "Frenchman Tasting a California Wine" by Guy Buffet available.
Please contact Far Niente for details. (707) 944-2861 ©1993 Far Niente Winery, Oakville, Californi

**FRENCH**
FREQUENT DINING & GIVING PROGRAM

# CITRONELLE

901 EAST CABRILLO BLVD.
AT MILPAS
SANTA BARBARA, CA 93102
(805) 963-0111
*Visa & Major Credit Cards*
*Open Daily • Lunch & Dinner*

*Co-Proprietor*
**LARRY SHUPNICK**

*Chef*
**MARTIAL NOGUIER**

## Menu Highlights

*Appetizers*
SCALLOPS WITH
CRISPY MAUI ONION RINGS
• SMOKED SALMON TERRINE
WITH CUCUMBER DILL SALAD
• SHIITAKE & GARLIC FEUILLETÉ

*Entrées*
CHICKEN WITH PORCINI CRUST,
RAGOUT OF MUSHROOM &
MUSHROOM SAUCE
• ROASTED MUSCOVY DUCK
WITH BORDELAISE FIG SAUCE
• GRILLED SWORDFISH
WITH FLAGEOLETS & SWEET
BASIL SAUCE

MASTER CHEF/OWNER MICHEL RICHARD OF CITRUS FAME HAS exported a version of that highly successful Los Angeles restaurant to Santa Barbara. Having recently opened a Citronelle in Baltimore and the nation's Capital, Richard chose the third floor of the Santa Barbara Inn for his flagship because of its magnificent view of the Santa Barbara coast. ♦ Based on the Citrus menu, Citronelle's dishes are also light and elegant. Parisian Chef Martial Noguier, who spent time at Patina and Citrus, oversees the kitchen with panache. His signature creations include yellowtail carpaccio with ginger vinaigrette and tuna tournedo with green pepper sauce. His equally notable prix-fixe dinner is a good opportunity for more extensive sampling. The wine list showcases the best of France and California. ♦ Michel Richard's Crunchy Napoleon laced with butterscotch is a delicious reminder that his desserts were first to bring him notoriety.

**AVERAGE DINNER FOR TWO: $64**
DOES NOT INCLUDE WINE, TAX AND GRATUITY

# EL ENCANTO

HOTEL AND GARDEN VILLAS
1900 LASUEN ROAD
SANTA BARBARA, CA 93103
(805) 687-5000

*Visa & Major Credit Cards*
*Open Daily • Lunch & Dinner*

*Maître d'*
DEMOS PETROPOULOS

*Chef*
GUY LEROY

## Menu Highlights

*Appetizers*

GARLIC FLAN WITH ROASTED HAZELNUTS • LEEK POTATO TART WITH BASIL CURED SALMON, RED & GOLDEN CAVIAR SOUR CREAM

*Entrées*

CONCHIGLIE PASTA WITH BOLLET, SHIITAKE & OYSTER MUSHROOMS, THYME FLOWERS • PAELLA WITH BLUE PRAWNS, CLAMS, MUSSELS, SEA SCALLOPS & OCTOPUS • GRILLED CHICKEN BREAST FILLED WITH GOAT CHEESE, CILANTRO LEAVES, SUNDRIED & ROMA TOMATOES

AS A MEMBER OF HISTORIC HOTELS OF AMERICA, EL ENCANTO Hotel and Garden Villas is a restored landmark hotel, sitting atop the "Santa Barbara Riviera" in a secluded wood on ten acres of lush, tropical gardens. It offers a magnificent view of the ocean below and unparalleled city views. With its romantic dining room and outdoor terrace, El Encanto resembles a Mediterranean villa in mood and design. ♦ The restaurant menu, created by Chef Guy Leroy, features the absolute freshest and finest regional products available at market and combines innovative California cuisine style with the flavors of the South of France. The fish at El Encanto is almost always from local waters and regional fruits, vegetables and herbs are the stars in Leroy's exquisitely presented dishes. Desserts include "Floating Island," a delicious and elegant creation of crème anglaise, meringue, caramel and almond.

**AVERAGE DINNER FOR TWO: $60**
DOES NOT INCLUDE WINE, TAX AND GRATUITY

146

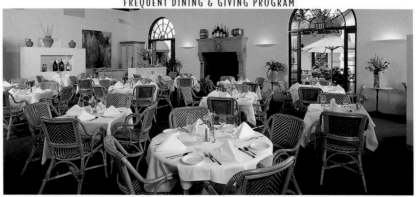

# WINE CASK

813 ANACAPA STREET
AT DE LA GUERRA
SANTA BARBARA, CA 93101
(805) 966-9463

*Visa & Major Credit Cards*
*Open Daily for Dinner • Lunch Mon-Fri*

| *Proprietor* | *Chef* |
| DOUGLAS MARGERUM | GALEN DOI |

## Menu Highlights

*Appetizers*

SHIITAKE MUSHROOM RISOTTO
WITH SHAVED PARMESAN
• FRIED RAVIOLI FILLED WITH
SPINACH, MUSHROOMS & BRIE

*Entrées*

GRILLED PESTO-STUFFED
SWORDFISH SERVED ON CREAMY
POLENTA WITH SUNDRIED
TOMATO BASIL SAUCE • GRILLED
SEA SCALLOPS IN WASABI SAUCE
WITH POTATO PANCAKE &
JULIENNE OF VEGETABLES
• HERB-CRUSTED COLORADO
LAMB LOIN IN ROASTED GARLIC
SAUCE, POTATO GRATIN

NESTLED IN THE HISTORIC DISTRICT OF EL PASEO IN DOWNTOWN Santa Barbara, the Wine Cask offers patrons a choice of dining al fresco in the delightful courtyard of this circa 1900 former residence, or in the Gold Room with its high, painted ceiling and baronial fireplace. Douglas Margerum has created a casual yet elegant atmosphere, his brother Hugh's impressionistic paintings in perfect harmony with the restaurant's 1920s interior. ♦ Chef Galen Doi, formerly of the Ritz-Carlton in Palm Springs and San Ysidro Ranch, brings a Japanese influence along with classic French training to his cuisine. Regional ingredients help him create an eclectic, California menu. "My passion for cooking," says Doi, "was passed on to me by my parents." His delicious roasted Muscovy duck "Amiko" with orange cumin sauce and ginger is actually his mother's recipe and named in her honor. ♦ Wine aficionados can either peruse the fifty-page wine list and choose from more than 2,000 selections.

**AVERAGE DINNER FOR TWO: $45**
DOES NOT INCLUDE WINE, TAX AND GRATUITY

# *Meadowood*
## Napa Valley

A World Apart in the Napa Valley

Fireplace Suites, The Grill,
The Restaurant, Tennis,
Golf, Croquet, Pools,
Hiking Trails, Wine School,
**The Health Spa**

Meadowood Resort • 900 Meadowood Lane • St. Helena, CA 94574
TEL (707) 963-3646  FAX (707) 963-3532

# WORLD CLASS WINES

## BY NORMAN ROBY

**A**S THE 1990s UNFOLD, THE QUALITY OF wine throughout the world has never been higher. Beginning in the 1960s, California upstarts challenged the French and Italian wine industries. Other states and other countries soon followed. After a decade of growth and experimentation in the 1970s, wines took a quantum leap as an international spirit of cooperation began. ◆ Today, winemakers from France, Italy and the United States regularly visit each other's cellars to exchange information and to collaborate on research projects. Without compromising the integrity of their own distinctive wine regions, they have created new approaches to grape growing and winemaking. The result: better wines and more choices than ever before.

# WINE TALK

PART OF THE ENJOYMENT OF WINES comes from the conversations they inspire. Quite often the subject is the wine itself. Talking about wine should be easy and relaxed. To help matters along, we have defined the most commonly used words and phrases, with particular emphasis on wine aromas. Most wine commentary proceeds by analogies and suggestions, so trust your instincts, offer your impressions and create descriptions.

◆ AROMA  All-purpose word for the smell of a wine, which may vary in type (fruity, floral, spicy) and in strength. Aroma is used in the general sense and is usually positive.

◆ ASTRINGENT  The sensation of a wine that leaves a puckery feel in the mouth and seems to dry out the palate. Most young Cabernets and Zinfan-dels are astringent. Tannins, from the grapes and oak barrels, contribute to astringency, which is more common in red wines.

**MERIDIAN**™

Taste the
Art of Chardonnay
from the
Santa Barbara Coast

♦ AUSTERE  Characteristic of wines that are lean in body and high in acidity but overall on the pleasant side. Usually white wines are likely to be austere in style.

♦ BALANCED  When all of a wine's components (fruit, alcohol, acidity, tannin, oak, sweetness) exist in a harmonious way, the wine is said to be balanced.

♦ BERRYLIKE  Common aroma description for wines with a fairly distinct fruit character. Zinfandels are often similar to blackberries, Cabernets to black currants and Pinot Noirs to cherries.

♦ BODY  The relative weight of a wine or its viscosity. Ranges from thin to light, to medium, to full-bodied. How a wine clings to the sides of a glass when you swirl it is an indication of its body.

♦ BOUQUET  The odors developed through the aging process as distinguished from the fruity/spicy aroma of the grape.

♦ COMPLEX  Describes both aromas and flavors, and the existence of several facets simultaneously. Multidimensional wines are complex. The opposite style is simple or one-dimensional.

♦ CRISP  Wines that are lively on the palate and leave you with a lip-smacking impression similar to tart. Usually results from relatively high acidity.

♦ DRY  Basically, the opposite of sweet.

♦ EARTHY  Exists in varying degrees, from a subtle aroma of dusty weediness to a pungent aroma of mushrooms and truffles. More commonly found in red wines.

♦ FLORAL  Aromas similar to flowers in bloom are said to be floral. White wines such as Johannisberg Riesling and Gewurztraminer are often floral with hints of jasmine and orange blossom. The aroma of violets and roses exists in some Pinot Noirs.

- GRASSY  A fresh, lively aroma reminiscent of freshly cut grass, usually considered pleasant, and characteristic of many Sauvignon Blancs. Some Chardonnays and a few Chenin Blancs can be grassy.

- HERBACEOUS/HERBAL  Collective terms for aromas hinting of dried herbs such as sage, dill and mint. Herbaceousness is most often found in Sauvignon Blanc.

- HONEY  An enticing sweet smell present in some white wines. It is usually a result of *Botrytis cinerea,* "the noble rot."

- NOSE  The combination of all odors, aroma, bouquet, oak, etc., detected by the olfactory sense.

- OAKED  The aroma derived directly from oak barrel aging and usually described as vanillalike. The oak is fired to conform to the barrel shape.

- SMOKY  An aroma derived mostly from fired oak barrels and often perceived as toasty or roasted, similar to the smell of burning leaves.

- SPICY  Many fine wines are characteristically spicy, suggesting cloves, cinnamon and pepper. Zinfandel and Syrah wines tend to be peppery; among white wines, Gewurztraminer can be very spicy.

- SUPPLE  A wine that is extremely subtle in a soft, smooth style without being heavy in body.

- VEGETATIVE  This covers a range of aromas, from the quite attractive smell of green olives and bell peppers often common to Cabernet Sauvignon and Sauvignon Blanc, to the less attractive green bean and asparagus smells sometimes detected in both types of wine.

- YEASTY  An aroma similar to fresh-baked bread, highly desirable in Champagne and sparkling wines. Some white wines, notably Chardonnay and Sauvignon Blanc, are aged in contact with yeasty and acquire a subtle yeastiness. ■

A Century Of Styl
And Innovation

# Jordan

ELEGANCE IN A BOTTLE

# CALIFORNIA WINES

C ALIFORNIA WINES HAVE DEFINITELY COME of age. The finest are now being collected, coveted and cellared with the zeal once reserved for prestigious European wines. Perhaps even more telling is the way trendsetting restaurants now proudly offer an array of California wines. ◆ European wine producers have bestowed the ultimate compliment on California as a prime wine region by choosing to become a part of the excitement. Companies such as Moët et Chandon, Piper, Pommery, Roederer, Mouton-Rothschild, Taittinger, G.H. Mumm, Freixenet and many others have joined the dynamic California wine world. ◆ With more than 700 wineries in existence and others on the way, no winery will be able to rest on its laurels. As good as California wines are today, the overall quality level will only continue to rise.

NORTH
COAST
NAPA
VALLEY
SONOMA
VALLEY
San
Francisco
Sacramento
SIERRA
FOOTHILLS
CENTRAL
COAST
Los Angeles
TEMECULA
San Diego

CALIFORNIA
VITICULTURAL
AREAS

# ARIÉL

The Premium Wines Without Alcohol

**ARIÉL**

**Cabernet Sauvignon**
PREMIUM DEALCOHOLIZED WINE

## NORM ROBY RECOMMENDS

### SPARKLING WINES

BY THE LATE 1980s, CALIFORNIA SPARKLING wines earned international acceptance. Much of the credit for this goes to the influence of the French contingent: Moët et Chandon, Piper-Heidsieck, Mumm, Roederer and Pommery. But the pioneering efforts of hometown favorites such as Schramsberg, Korbel and Iron Horse should not go unnoticed. ♦ The finest sparkling wine producers use the traditional *méthode champenoise,* but do not try to imitate French Champagne. Instead, they produce California sparkling wine with a distinct personality and an exciting fruit accent.

MUMM NAPA VALLEY: From its ever-popular Napa Brut Prestige to its ultra-premium Vintage Reserve and special "Winery Lake Cuvée," Mumm Napa Valley is now considered one of California's premier *méthode champenoise* producers.

IRON HORSE VINEYARDS: Owners Barry and Audrey Sterling selected the cool Green Valley area for sparkling wines. Both the Brut and Blanc de Blancs are rich, crisp, perfectly rendered versions.

DOMAINE CHANDON: Since the 1970s, Chandon has paved the way with its Brut and Blanc de Noirs. Now its complex, toasty Reserve ranks among the best ever. Chandon also owns the popular Shadow Creek line.

ROEDERER ESTATE: This handsome Anderson Valley newcomer makes only one sparkler, a Brut as refined and lovely as any. Mature oak-aged wine is added for extra interest.

SCHARFFENBERGER: This Anderson Valley producer's finest wine, the Blanc de Blanc, is crisp and lovely. Pale straw in color, their sparkling wine has fine bubbles, a distinctly varietal nose and a long finish.

SCHRAMSBERG VINEYARDS: Pioneers Jamie and Jack Davies toiled for years, for good cause. Their Cuvée de Pinot is a sensational, serious Rosé; the toasty Blanc de Blancs, a rare treat.

JORDAN WINERY: The result of extensive research, Jordan's entry into the field is effusively bubbly with a creamy texture and complex aroma of fruit and yeastiness.

DOMAINE CARNEROS: This exciting and sophisticated first effort from Taittinger's Carneros outpost is remarkably rich and bold in Brut style. ∎

154

SAUVIGNON BLANC IS ON THE VERGE OF becoming California's best all-around white wine. The grape adapts to a wide range of soils and climates, preferring slightly warm to cool temperatures. Winemakers love to experiment with different styles of Sauvignon Blanc by altering the oak-aging routine or by using Semillon as a body-builder. The end result is a wonderful diversity.

CAKEBREAD CELLARS: The Cakebread family has worked long and hard to convince the world that Sauvignon Blanc is a first-class wine. By the end of the 1980s, theirs had become a model of beauty and complexity.

MATANZAS CREEK WINERY: For years, this winery has turned out focused, beautifully crafted Sauvignon Blancs that age well, yet are also delicious upon release. They are unusually rich on the palate.

SILVERADO VINEYARDS: Restrained in varietal grassiness, this wine is otherwise a treasure chest of ripe, juicy, fruity flavors.

KENWOOD VINEYARDS: In the winner's circle every year since 1983, Kenwood favors an intense grassy/weedy style that is magically controlled to produce round, smooth flavors.

DRY CREEK VINEYARD: Owner David Stare practically defined the fresh-cut grass, medium-bodied, focused style of Fumé Blanc from Sonoma County. Recent vintages contain a subtle oak component.

WILLIAM WHEELER WINERY: Blending wines from several Sonoma County appellations, winemaker Julia Iantosca has been quietly succeeding with wines of subtlety, richness and unusually brisk acidity.

HANNA WINERY: A pretty wine from an unusual label, Hanna's Sauvignon Blanc is herbal in aroma and smooth in texture. Aged for several months in new French oak, it is luscious on the palate.

SIMI WINERY: Under Zelma Long's guidance, Simi's Sauvignon Blanc is subtle and stylish, with depth and a lingering finish. ∎

Beringer.
CHARDONNAY
NAPA VALLEY

1991

Beringer
CHARDONNAY
NAPA VALLEY
*Proprietor Grown*

Beringer Vineyards, St. Helena, California

CHARDONNAY, THE WORLD'S GREATEST WHITE wine, has almost become a victim of its own popularity. Just about every winery in and out of California now bottles a Chardonnay — with predictably uneven results. Whether made in a crisp apple, medium-bodied style, or an oak-enhanced, buttery smooth, tropical fruit style, California's leading Chardonnays are more refined and better balanced today than they were a decade ago.

MERIDIAN VINEYARDS: Winemaker Chuck Ortman combines rich, tropical fruit with lush, creamy oak, and in 1991 produced a full-bodied, stellar example of Central Coast Chardonnay.

KISTLER VINEYARDS: Winemakers Steve Kistler and Mark Bixler have recently produced stunning, unbeatable Chardonnays. From their small winery in the Sonoma Valley, they make an Estate Chardonnay as well as three other beauties: McCrea Vineyard, Dutton Ranch and Durell Vineyard.

MATANZAS CREEK WINERY: Sandra and Bill MacIver's wines have been a marvel of consistency and quality since they opened their winery in the Bennett Valley. They are rich, complex and superbly balanced.

CUVAISON WINERY: Once Cuvaison's Carneros vineyards were in full production, winemaker John Thatcher launched a series of elegant, silky, soft Chardonnays that are a sheer delight.

CHATEAU MONTELENA: Montelena ranks among the top Chardonnays in all of California. Winemaker Bo Barrett has an unblemished Chardonnay record.

GRGICH HILLS: Mike Grgich continues his winning ways with Chardonnay from his own winery. Since 1977, he has put his stamp on wines of great varietal character and harmony.

BERINGER VINEYARDS: Beringer's pleasing style, as evidenced by the '91, focuses on fresh apple fruit, subtle oak notes, and substantial flavors with impeccable balance.

BURGESS: Tom Burgess relies on his own Triere Vineyard in Yountville for his Chardonnays, produced in the classic winemaking style of white Burgundies.

KENDALL JACKSON WINERY: This Lake County winery's owner, Jess Jackson, prefers to blend grapes from several of California's coastal growing regions for his balanced, refined Chardonnays.

FAR NIENTE VINEYARDS: Recent vintages from this winery are now barrel-fermented and aged in technologically designed wine caves. The Chardonnay is known for its beautiful balance, long finish and consistent quality.

## CHARDONNAY

**CLOS DU BOIS:** A winery with several fine Chardonnays, Clos du Bois makes one from the Calcaire Vineyard that is often mistaken for a great French wine.

**CHATEAU ST. JEAN:** A leader since its first vintage, St. Jean has been a marvel of consistency with its well-knit Chardonnays. The Belle Terre remains one of the richest of all vineyard designates.

**TREFETHEN VINEYARDS:** With pert, apple fruit and subtle oak, this Chardonnay is beautifully balanced. Silky and gossamer in texture, it drinks well early on but also ages gracefully.

**SIMI WINERY:** Using grapes from Sonoma and Mendocino, Simi keeps pace with the fast pack. Its silky smooth, well-knit regular Chardonnay improves each year, and its Reserve is as rich as Chardonnay can be.

**FERRARI CARANO WINERY:** Intricate and compact in structure, the '91 Alexander Valley possesses deep, intense fruit flavors along with lovely oak nuances. The wine is complex in style without being heavy-handed.

**MERRYVALE VINEYARDS:** Specializing in two wines, Merryvale buys grapes from the most famous growers in Napa Valley. The Chardonnay, aged in new French oak, has been outstanding in recent vintages.

**SONOMA CUTRER:** From its well-focused, enjoyable "Russian River Ranches" to its intense, complex "Les Pierres" bottling, this winery has ranked near the top since its inception.

**DE LOACH VINEYARDS:** Always effusively fruity and appealing when young, De Loach Chardonnays are marvelously sophisticated with rich flavors and a silky smooth texture.

**J. LOHR ESTATES:** The Riverstone from Monterey displays sprightly apple and spice character and is round and smooth in the finish. This seamless package comes complete with a touch of oak and balancing acidity.

**RAYMOND VINEYARD:** This winery has a knack for making wines that please the palate. With medium oak, the Napa Valley Chardonnays capture peach and apple flavors and are rich and supple on the palate.

**JORDAN VINEYARDS:** Showing direct influences of barrel fermentation, Jordan's compact, restrained versions are full-bodied and greatly resemble fine Burgundian counterparts.

**VICHON COASTAL SELECTIONS:** The wizardry of Robert Mondavi shines through in this intensely fruity, lively styled wine that offers great varietal character and value.

**FETZER VINEYARDS:** Upgraded to the big league, the '92 Barrel Select delivers well-defined apple fruit, rich, chunky flavors and plenty of oak complexity. ∎

A WINE LOVER'S WINE, PINOT NOIR IS POSSIBLY an acquired taste. But since it is demanding to grow and insists on cool locations, fine Pinot Noir will never be available in enormous quantities. So far the best Pinot Noir is coming from four cool locales — the Carneros District, Sonoma's Russian River Valley, Mendocino's Anderson Valley and Santa Barbara County. At its finest, Pinot Noir is light in color, full in body, velvety in texture, and reminiscent of smoky cherries — sometimes with a hint of beef, bacon and mushrooms. It sounds like a strange mix, but Pinot Noir is a wine of contrasts.

ACACIA WINERY: Now part of the Chalone family, Acacia continues its champion ways with multiple bottlings. For true cherry-like character and velvety texture, the St. Clair bottling is tops.

DEHLINGER WINERY: Winemaker Tom Dehlinger, a perfectionist among perfectionists, is making waves with a rich style of Pinot Noir that emphasizes cherries and spices.

CARNEROS CREEK WINERY: Much of the credit for improved Pinot Noir in California should go to Francis Mahoney, whose experimental vineyard has proven invaluable. His own bottlings from the Carneros are among the richest and ripest, yet also among the most supple.

CALERA: All of Calera's Pinot Noirs are intense, concentrated and long-lived. Calera produces four distinct, single-vineyard Pinots from their limestone soils on Mt. Harlan, as well as a "Central Coast" Pinot Noir made from purchased grapes.

SAINTSBURY: Dick Ward and David Graves capture the sleek, satiny, pure cherry character from the Carneros region. Year after year, theirs is one of the best balanced Pinots.

WILD HORSE WINERY: Ken Volk's winery is in Templeton, but he selects from the finest growers in Santa Barbara to offer a rich style of Pinot Noir that reminds many experts of a fine Côte de Nuits.

BUENA VISTA: One of the oldest names in California, Buena Vista has an extraordinary 1,000-acre vineyard in the Carneros. From it, Jill Davis makes a delicate but varietally correct Pinot Noir, with charm, subtlety and just the right degree of toasty oak.

STERLING VINEYARDS: From the legendary Winery Lake Vineyard in the Carneros District, Sterling's rendition opts for subtle cherry fruit, enriching oak and overall elegance. ∎

THE GRAPE OF THE FABLED POMEROL, Merlot attracted belated interest from growers and wine-makers in the late 1960s. Since then, Merlot has dramatically increased in stature among consumers and in importance among collectors. At its best, Merlot offers depth along with a mouth-filling, mouth-coating texture, and an aroma of herbs, spices, cherries and black currants.

**DUCKHORN VINEYARD:** The pacesetter for Merlot since 1978, winemaker Tom Rinaldi calls Duckhorn's Three Palms the most intense, Vine Hill the next in line, and Napa Valley the first to enjoy.

**MATANZAS CREEK VINEYARD:** From Sonoma County, this Merlot rises above the rest because of its incredible richness and finesse. With an aroma of spices and herbs, it has enough tannin to age long and well.

**MARKHAM VINEYARDS:** One of the best-kept secrets of the 1980s, Markham's Merlots are beautifully balanced, with just the right degree of sweet oak, soft tannin and varietal intensity.

**CUVAISON WINERY:** Emerging as a class winery in the 1980s, Cuvaison achieved tremendous success with Merlot. Aromas of cedar and fruit combine with ripeness and smooth oak in this voluptuous rendition.

**FRANCISCAN OAKVILLE ESTATE:** Franciscan has offered velvety smooth Merlots with plenty of spicy, jammy varietal fruit since the early 1980s. Excellent depth assures good cellaring potential.

**STERLING VINEYARDS:** Among the first producers of Merlot, Sterling now favors finesse and elegance in style. The aroma typically combines berries and herbaceousness in a distinctive, medium-intense version.

**CLOS PEGASE:** Supple, smooth Merlots with just the right degree of tannic backbone have quickly carved out a niche for this new label.

**GUNDLACH BUNDSCHU:** From their Rhinefarm Vineyard, the Bundschus make one of the few genuine, full-bodied, ripe-styled Merlots.

**BENZIGER WINERY:** Lush berry flavors, oak richness and wonderful aromatics make this version appealing in its youth.

**VICHON WINERY:** Owned by Robert Mondavi's three children, Vichon is making rich, complex Merlot on the same high level as all Mondavi-influenced reds. ∎

*Fine wine exclusively crafted from the Trefethen family's Napa Valley estate. Open, pour, sip, savor.*

*One of the best.*

WITHOUT QUESTION, CABERNET SAUVIGNON has been California's greatest wine for at least thirty years. Now, with more producers and furious competition, the overall quality is better than ever. Winemakers have become more skilled at their trade, using blenders such as Cabernet Franc and/or Merlot when they feel a more exciting wine will result. At the same time, experienced winemakers who began in the 1970s are applying their accumulated wisdom to produce more subtle, elegant and restrained Cabernets. All three factors come into play in the best vintages of the 1980s — '85, '86 and '87.

FAR NIENTE: In the magnificently refurbished winery, Far Niente turns out Cabernet Sauvignons that have become highly sought after. Made from Napa Valley grapes, Far Niente Cabernets are rich, full and well-balanced for aging. Their soft tannins also permit them to be enjoyed young.

CAYMUS VINEYARDS: Winemaker Chuck Wagner has the Midas touch with Cabernet. The rare Special Selection is superb and long-lived, but the Estate Bottled is always outstanding. Even the Napa Cuvée is special.

SILVER OAK CELLARS: A Cabernet specialist, Silver Oak ages its wines in cask and bottle until they are fully developed and smooth. As a result, the Alexander Valley bottling and the Napa Valley version are so beautiful they should be on every fine wine list.

BEAULIEU VINEYARD: One of the benchmarks of Napa Valley Cabernet, the winery's Private Reserve continues to rank high on every collector's list. Ripe, earthy and tannic, it ages well.

ROBERT MONDAVI WINERY: Both the regular bottling and the Reserve improve a little each year and remain among the best of their price category. Held for three years in new French oak, the recent Reserves have exceeded all expectations.

BERINGER VINEYARDS: This venerable Napa Valley name has been making truly distinctive, top-notch Reserve Cabernets since the late 1970s. Selecting from the finest Napa grapes, Beringer's winemaster, Ed Sbragia, has been on a roll since 1984.

DUNN VINEYARDS: Randy Dunn (formerly of Caymus) founded a small winery on Howell Mountain in 1979. Every vintage since then has been coveted by collectors. Both the Howell Mountain and Napa Valley Cabernets are fabulous.

CLOS DU VAL: Located along the Silverado Trail, Clos du Val was among the first to show the potential of the Stags Leap district. Winemaster Bernard Portet's supple Cabernets reveal the French influence.

**RAYMOND VINEYARDS:** The Raymonds quietly go about making quality Cabernets, then let the wines do the talking. Their Private Reserves and regular Napa Valley bottlings are textbook perfect.

**STERLING VINEYARDS:** Long a favorite among collectors, Sterling's Reserves are sturdy and slow to reach maturity, but heavenly wines for those who can wait.

**JOSEPH PHELPS VINEYARDS:** With aromas of ripe berries, spice and pepper, Phelps' Cabernets are normally supple and well-proportioned. The '90 Napa Valley reflects greater intensity.

**JORDAN VINEYARDS:** The epitome of style and grace, these Cabernets are rich and mouthfilling. They showcase the berry and cedar character of the Alexander Valley in a smooth, refined package.

**RIDGE VINEYARDS:** Arguably the most distinctive and long-lived of all California Cabernets, Ridge's Monte Bello is packed with black currant, earthy and spicy components, as well as considerable tannin for aging.

**VICHON COASTAL SELECTIONS:** Widely praised for offering value, this Cabernet, blending the best from the North and Central Coast regions, managed to be varietally correct and versatile.

**ST. CLEMENT VINEYARDS:** Well-knit, with perfect balance, the Cabernets from St. Clement are amazingly harmonious and consistently excellent. Their aromas of currants and herbs are the essence of Cabernet.

**SILVERADO VINEYARDS:** Carving out a new style of Cabernet, winemaker Jack Stuart emphasizes fruit and soft tannins in his wines. Though accessible when young, they will reward cellaring.

**GROTH VINEYARDS:** Producing one of the most sought-after Reserves, Groth also makes a turbo-charged Napa Valley Cabernet that is packed with intense, ripe fruit and built to last.

**CHARLES KRUG WINERY:** Its '85 vintage selection signals a return to top form for this fabled Napa Valley name.

**BURGESS CELLARS:** The Vintage Selection Cabernets from Burgess are so consistently fine that they deserve even more praise than they receive. From old mountain vineyards in Napa, they age well.

**RODNEY STRONG WINERY:** Its "Alexander's Crown" was among the first single-vineyard Cabernets and remains among the most collectible.

**FETZER VINEYARDS:** Popular for its Barrel Select Cabernets, this admired family winery has a Reserve that is now winning over collectors. ■

# VICHON
# COASTAL

Our Coastal wines combine
the rich, bright fruit of
Santa Barbara County with
the elegance and depth of
Napa Valley.

Try a bottle of our
Coastal Chardonnay or Cabernet
Sauvignon with dinner tonight.

VICHON
*is a proud sponsor of Meals on Wheels.*

A FAIRLY NEW VARIETAL FOR CALIFORNIA winemakers, Syrah is a major grape of the expanding red varietals. When winemakers learned that an old workhorse grape named Petite Sirah was unrelated to the French Syrah, several decided to try it. California winemakers depend extensively on the French knowledge of this grape, little known in America. The Syrah thrives in the Rhône Valley of France where it is converted into sturdy but heavenly wines such as Côte Rotie, Hermitage and Cornas. The wines offer an intriguing aroma of black pepper, green olives and plenty of spice. Generally subtle and medium in tannins, Syrah wines can last for many years.

JOSEPH PHELPS VINEYARDS: After a few trial vintages with the Syrah, Phelps hit paydirt in 1982 and has become one of the driving forces from that time forward with wine that is perfumed, liquid satin.

ZACA MESA WINERY: In 1983, Santa Ynez Valley winemaker Ken Brown produced a modest quantity of his first vintage. This light, fruity and smooth to the palate varietal has a pleasant hint of butterscotch.

STAG'S LEAP WINE CELLARS: Owner Warren Winiarski is an artistic winemaker challenged to produce a beauty from Petite Sirah. The current vintages have brought out lovely berry-like fruit flavors and considerable charm.

McDOWELL VALLEY VINEYARDS: With the oldest Syrah plantings in California, McDowell turns out an intensely fruity, spicy wine that has remained a well-kept secret, until now.

RIDGE WINERY: Believing that the old Petite Sirah can yield a first-class wine, Ridge makes believers of us all through a recent vintage identified as "York Creek," a Napa vineyard owned by Fritz Maytag of Anchor Steam Beer fame.

DUXOUP WINEWORKS: Syrah grapes from Lou Preston's vineyards provide winemaker Andy Cutter with the harvest for his 185 cases of this smooth varietal. Fermented in redwood and oak aged, the wine is released young. The fruity character is well enhanced with the wood contact to present a velvety champion. ∎

ZINFANDEL HAS BEEN ON A FAST ROLLER-coaster ride since being discovered in the late 1960s. As the '90s unfold, it is again on top as a highly esteemed red dinner wine that is a remarkably versatile food companion. The roster of producers has changed many times, and only those firmly committed to Zinfandel as a serious, sophisticated wine continue to offer it. The appellations emerging as excellent for Zinfandel are Dry Creek Valley, Mendocino, Sonoma Valley, Howell Mountain and other Napa Valley hillside regions.

RIDGE VINEYARDS: For more than twenty vintages, Ridge has shown the way by offering Zinfandels from several appellations. The Geyserville is massive and handsome, the Lytton Springs a close second.

STORYBOOK MOUNTAIN: A Zinfandel specialist located north of Calistoga, Storybook offers a Napa Valley and an Estate Reserve Zinfandel. Both are elegant, balanced wines capable of long aging.

FETZER VINEYARDS: A longtime advocate of Zinfandel from Mendocino County, Fetzer makes a Ricetti Reserve and a Mendocino Reserve. Both display a strawberry, spicy character.

CHATEAU SOUVERAIN: After its major renovation phase, this winery has focused on its wines. Among the best is its Zinfandel from the Dry Creek Valley, a spicy, medium-bodied beauty.

QUIVIRA VINEYARDS: Another winner from Dry Creek, Quivira Zinfandel offers jammy fruit and good depth. It is superbly balanced.

BURGESS CELLARS: Since the early 1970s, Tom Burgess has made Zinfandels from other hillside vineyards in Napa Valley. His wines are very aromatic and berrylike.

RAVENSWOOD: Joel Peterson is a Zinfandel fanatic. He offers a Sonoma County, a Dickerson and a Vintner's Blend, all complex and rich.

LYTTON SPRINGS WINERY: Using vineyards planted in 1900, Lytton Springs produces big, intense, ripe Zinfandels with tremendous flavor concentration. They are the epitome of Sonoma Zinfandel.

CLOS DU VAL: French-born winemaster Bernard Portet works with Zinfandel to capture the berry and spice character of the grape in a refined, medium-bodied French style.

BERINGER VINEYARDS: Loaded with sweet fruit and enticing spices, this wine offers sheer pleasure to Zinfandel fanatics. Its appellation is North Coast; its character one-of-a-kind.

KENWOOD VINEYARDS: Always on target, Kenwood has added a Zinfandel from the Jack London Ranch that competes with its highly successful Sonoma Valley version. Both offer lovely fruit flavors. ■

# FETZER™
### VINEYARDS

*from the earth to the table*℠

Groth

NAPA VALLEY

*Cabernet Sauvignon*
*Chardonnay*
*Sauvignon Blanc*

THE BEST
IT CAN GET.

IN THE 1980s MANY CALIFORNIA WINEMAKERS became intrigued by Bordeaux wines and began trying to replicate those famous clarets. By combining Cabernet Sauvignon with Merlot, Cabernet Franc and — when available — Malbec and Petit Verdot, winemakers created a type of wine unlike any one varietal. Before too long, an entirely new category of wine was created from traditional Bordeaux varieties and christened "Méritage."

OPUS ONE: The result of the partnership between the Robert Mondavi Winery and Château Mouton-Rothschild, Opus One made its debut in 1979. Ever since, this rich, super-refined wine has been ferreted away by collectors aware of its long-term aging ability.

CAIN FIVE: As soon as they started their winery in 1981, Joyce and Jerry Cain decided to create this red from the five Bordeaux grapes. Since its 1985 inaugural wine, Cain Five has been highly acclaimed.

INSIGNIA: First made in 1974, Insignia from Joseph Phelps Vineyards was the California pioneer of the type. This style tends to display cedar and currants in the aroma, richness and suppleness in the flavors.

LYETH WINERY: Since 1981, Lyeth has exclusively produced an elegant and highly acclaimed Bordeaux-styled red wine from the Alexander Valley.

MARLSTONE: Entered by Clos du Bois, Marlstone has ranked among the best for elegance and sheer beauty since it was introduced in 1978.

MERRYVALE: Using grapes from pedigreed Napa Valley Vineyards, the owners of Merryvale, who also own the Sunny St. Helena Winery, produce only Chardonnay and this rich, long-lived red, blended from Cabernet Sauvignon, Merlot and Cabernet Franc.

TRILOGY: Made from three grapes — Cabernet Sauvignon, Merlot and Cabernet Franc — Trilogy is the pride of Flora Springs. Its owners select from their estate vineyards in Rutherford to produce this compact, limited-volume, well-knit Méritage blend.

OAKVILLE ESTATE MÉRITAGE: From Franciscan Vineyards, this relative newcomer, a blend of Cabernet Sauvignon and Merlot, is round on the palate, but boasts a powerful scent of fruit, oak and spice. ■

DESSERT-STYLE WINES GENERALLY FALL INTO two distinct types. The first includes wines labeled Late Harvest or something similar — most often made from Riesling or Semillon and, occasionally, from Sauvignon Blanc. *Botrytis cinerea*, a naturally occurring mold, concentrates the grape sugars and imparts exotic fragrances and flavors. These wines depend on natural conditions and are not produced every year. ♦ The second type of dessert wine, typified by Sherry, Port and Madeira, is fortified by the addition of grape spirits and produced every year.

LATE HARVEST RIESLINGS: Since the mid-1970s, Château St. Jean and Joseph Phelps have led the way with often stunning Late Harvest and Select Late Harvest Rieslings. Freemark Abbey's rich Edelwein Gold is intensely special. Other standouts are Hogue Cellars and Château Ste. Michelle from Washington State, and Hidden Cellars, Renaissance Vineyards and Navarro from California.

SPECIAL MUSCAT WINES: One of the most ancient wines, Muscat de Frontignan is a rare treat, best exemplified today by Beaulieu Vineyard's oak-aged Muscat de Frontignan. Quady Winery makes two tantalizing, lightly fortified wines: a decadent dessert wine named Essencia, and the enchanting Elysium, made from Black Muscat. For decades, one truly special wine named Moscato, a delicate, opulent, frothy wine, has come from Louis M. Martini.

PORT WINES: This deep, full-flavored fortified wine is usually enjoyed after a meal. From Portugal come fine Vintage Ports that require cellaring for a minimum of ten years, but preferably twenty. The sought-after brands today are Warre, Fonseca, Cockburn, Sandeman, Croft, Graham's, Dow and Taylor. Those upholding the Port tradition in California are Shenandoah Vineyards, J.W. Morris (try the Vintage Port), and Quady Winery, with its Vintage Port and Port of the Vintage.

MADEIRA: An island west of Morocco, Madeira give its name to one of the world's most authentic legends. Fortified and aged under warm, controlled conditions, Madeira, a favorite among colonial Americans, lives splendidly — well beyond a century. Rarely vintaged today, it is presented in four styles: Malmsey, Bual, Verdelho, and Sercial.

DOLCE: Modeled upon the finest French Sauternes, Dolce quickly rivaled them for sheer hedonistic pleasure. Full-bodied and unctuous, it can be enjoyed by itself as a perfect dessert. ■

# LEAVE NO STONE UNTURNED

*In Our Case, Consistency is Never Boring*

**J. Lohr Winery  1000 Lenzen Avenue
San Jose, California   95126  (408) 288-5057**

THE MEDOC GRANDS CRUS CLASSES OF 185⸱

# FRENCH WINES

T HE FRENCH HAVE BEEN MAKING WINE for centuries. They also set the standard in both quality and volume, and today produce nearly two billion gallons a year. ◆ The first lesson in understanding European wines is how they are identified. Unlike California wines, which are labeled by producer and varietal, French wines stress where the grapes originated — the appellation of origin. Most French wines are identified by region, such as Chablis or Bordeaux. ◆ The flavors and aromas of the wines mirror their growing region and climate, or their *terroir*, the French term for soil or ground. Since French wine labels emphasize appellation of origin, the vintner's name may appear only in small print. ◆ Because appellation of origin is so important, the use of place names is strictly controlled by the French government. ◆ A second important consideration is vintage, the year the grapes were picked and made into wine. Maintaining the same quality and taste year after year is impossible, particularly since European vineyards are often in climates and sites difficult for grape plantings. ◆ As a result, the wines produced in a specific area can vary in unexpected ways. Very good years produce more intense, typical flavor.

# THE MEDOC CRUS CLASSES OF 1855

## (and of 1973 for the first crus)

Not only were the sixty one Médoc Crus Classés the first to represent the aristocracy of Bordeaux wine, they were also the first to produce wines coming from a particular terroir and bearing the name of this terroir, often associated with that of a famous proprietor. The Crus Classés are the creators of Château wines.

Indeed, their vineyards are practically always graced by a beautiful dwelling or an assortment of working buildings which architecturally justifies the term Château and which has become the emblem of their international prestige.

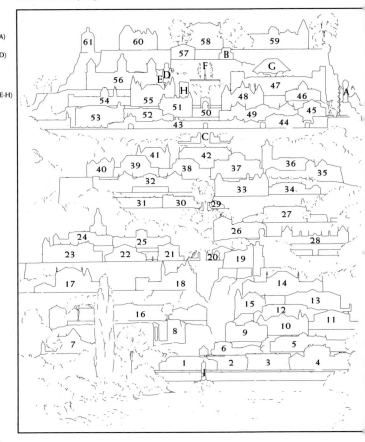

At the time of the "Châteaux-Bordeaux" Exhibition organized by the Georges Pompidou Centre in Paris, the architectural artist Carl LAUBIN had the idea of assembling on one single canvas the famous 1855 classification's 61 crus.

The numbers from 1 to 61 correspond to the principal buildings of each Cru Classé. In addition, Carl LAUBIN has drawn other architectural aspects associated with certain châteaux, these being identified by letters.

Posters of this painting are available in 60 x 84 cm size (Price: France and EEC: 45 FF - Other countries: 50 FF) by contacting:

CONSEIL DES CRUS CLASSES DU MEDOC. 1, cours du XXX-Juillet - 33000 BORDEAUX - FRANCE. Tél. 56 48 18 62 - Fax 56 79 11 05.

EVEN THE CASUAL AMERICAN wine-lover has become an avid collector of red Bordeaux, also known as Claret. To create Bordeaux, the winemaker blends Cabernet Sauvignon, Merlot, Cabernet Franc, Malbec and Petit Verdot grapes into whatever combination will yield the best of the vintage. A 260,000-acre appellation, Bordeaux is divided into many sub-appellations.

## RED BORDEAUX

**ST. ESTÈPHE:** Once synonymous with rough, slow-developing wines, St. Estèphe has been offering redesigned wines since about 1982. Typically ripe, rich and concentrated, they now have a welcome elegance and accessibility. While the established châteaux of Cos d'Estournel, Montrose and Calon-Ségur remain at the top, challengers include Les Ormes de Pez, de Pez, Phelan-Ségur, Haut-Marbuzet, Le Crock and Meyney.

**PAUILLAC:** Home to three legendary First Growths, Lafite, Latour and Mouton-Rothschild, Pauillac is famous for wines that combine intensity of flavor (cassis, cedar, berries) with finesse and subtlety. These characteristics are worshipped by collectors, envied by fellow wine producers, and duplicated by no one. Other châteaux names to look for include Pichon-Lalande, Pichon-Longueville-Baron, Lynch-Bages, Grand-Puy-Lacoste and Haut Batailley.

**ST. JULIEN:** Refined and subtle, the St. Juliens have just enough concentration to appeal to those who like richness. The finest can age long and well. The stars are Ducru-Beaucaillou, Léoville-Las-Cases, Léoville-Barton and Beychevelle; rapidly rising châteaux include Gruaud-Larose, Léoville-Poyferré and Talbot. Ever consistent is Langoa-Barton.

**MARGAUX:** Since the 1980s, the wine with more finesse than all the others comes from the town of Margaux and has been labeled Château Margaux. Among other châteaux bringing honor to the small Margaux appellation are Palmer, Angludet, Giscours, du Tertre, Prieuré-Lichine, Siran, La Tour de Mons, Monbrison, Malescot-St. Exupéry, Rausan-Ségla and Brane-Cantenac.

**HAUT MÉDOC:** In the same area as the famous Bordeaux towns, the Haut Médoc region is a large appellation that produces many fine wines of outstanding value. The top name is La Lagune, followed by Cantemerle, Sociando-Mallet, Camensac and Château Citran.

**MÉDOC:** Located in the northern area once known as the Bas Médoc, this region supplies many pleasant, early-maturing Clarets. Potensac, La Tour de By, Plagnac, La Cardonne and Moulin Rouge provide quality wines to enjoy while prize vintages remain in the cellar.

**ST. EMILION:** Overall, the large St. Emilion region is responsible for most of the great values from Bordeaux. The typical version blends Merlot and Cabernet Franc grapes with a dollop of Cabernet Sauvignon. Not abrasively tannic, St. Emilion wines are enjoyable when young. Ausone and Cheval Blanc are famous and priced accordingly; more price-sensitive are L'Angélus, Beauséjour-Bécot, Canon, Canon La Gaffelière, Pavie Decesse and Grand-Pontet.

**PESSAC-LÉOGNAN (GRAVES):** Home to Haut-Brion and La Mission Haut-Brion, Graves is located south of Bordeaux and yields many good to excellent wines, both red and white. For the reds, renewed enthusiasm is being directed toward Pape-Clément, De Fieuzal, Domaine de Chevalier, La Tour-Martillac, Haut-Bailly and La Louvière, exciting in 1988 and '89.

**POMEROL:** Made famous by Château Pétrus, Pomerol is a small appellation adjacent to St. Emilion. The soft, round Merlot grape figures prominently in Pomerol's wines, which enjoyed unusually strong demand in the 1980s. Along with Pétrus are Lafleur, Vieux Château Certan, Clinet, Certan de May, L'Evangile, de Sales, Le Pin, Le Bon Pasteur and Clos René.

## WHITE BORDEAUX

**PESSAC-LÉOGNAN (GRAVES):** This newly created appellation was carved out of Graves and contains most of the famous estates. Recently great strides have been made by two historic names, Château Carbonnieux and Domaine de Chevalier, La Tour-Martillac and De Fieuzal. Other well-balanced white wines come from Malartic-Lagravière, Olivier, La Louvière, Couhins-Lurton and de Cruzeau. Château Haut-Brion and Château Laville-Haut-Brion are two rare whites deserving separate mention.

**ENTRE-DEUX-MERS:** Light, crisp and refreshing are typical characteristics of the new and improved white wines under this name. Most of what is sold as "Bordeaux Blanc" has been redefined as Entre-Deux-Mers.

**SAUTERNES:** Sauternes is a wonder of nature made possible by the noble rot. Because of the risks and extra labor involved, Sauternes is the world's most expensive wine to produce. As always, Château d'Yquem is the top name — and it is heaven. Many others are making serious Sauternes, including Château Suduiraut, Rieussec, Climens, Filhot, Sigalas Rabaud and Lafaurie-Peyraguey. ∎

Château
Ducru-Beaucaillou

*Grand Cru Classé*
Saint-Julien

RUNNING SOME 600 MILES FROM EAST TO west, the Loire River traverses some of the most beautiful châteaux and wine country in all of France. Many of the wine estates are small in output and sell locally. The types of wine are surprisingly diverse, but the majority are white, with Rosé and sparkling wine both enjoying considerable success in the area.

SANCERRE: In the eastern Loire, Sancerre is close to Pouilly-Fumé, and both regions favor the Sauvignon Blanc for white wines. Sancerre wines are usually medium-bodied and tart, with extremely lively acidity. One of the standout producers is Paul Cotat, whose Sancerre "Chavignol" wines are fragrant and steely. Other fine producers of Sancerre are Château du Nozay, Vacheron, Lucien Thomas Archambault and P. Jolivet.

POUILLY-FUMÉ: The La Doucette name, which now dominates both production and quality, made Pouilly-Fumé famous. Often razor-sharp, the wines are very pungent in aroma, perfect with thick cheeses. They can also be aged for four to five years. The Masson-Blondelet name offers superb wines, as do Châtelain, Pascal, Jolivet and Castelac.

VOUVRAY: In the central part of the Loire, Vouvray is one of the most recognized Loire wines. The widely planted grape here is Chenin Blanc. The appellation allows for the making of both sparkling and non-sparkling wine, though Vouvray is generally regarded as non-sparkling. Both sweet and tart in the aftertaste, the typical Vouvray is a delightful match for many lightly seasoned dishes. For years, the Château de Moncontour has been the most widely enjoyed Vouvray; Marc Bredif is another reliable brand, along with Foreau, M. Martin, R. Loyau and Château de Montfort.

COTEAUX DU LAYON: An unusual sweet style that rarely leaves France, Coteaux du Layon is produced from Chenin Blanc grapes. But its distinctive style manifests itself through the appearance of the noble rot, *Botrytis cinerea*, for a wine scented of honey and spices. More powerful than a late harvest wine, it is not as rich and heavy as a Sauternes. One producer who sends a few cases to the States is Domaine Beaujeau.

MUSCADET: A large region in the western Loire, Muscadet is extremely cool. Originally from Burgundy, the grape that adapted well to the climate is now known as either the Melon or Muscadet variety. Widely available, Muscadets are dry, crisp and light- to medium-bodied. Though not wines to cellar, they are sturdy and complement shellfish beautifully. Those labeled "*Sur Lie*" were aged in contact with their yeast cells to acquire more flavors and to soften their acidity. Standouts are the Château du Cléray, Domaine Quilla, Meurgey and Domaine de la Batardière. ∎

A ONCE NEGLECTED REGION IN SOUTHEAST-ern france, the Rhône Valley soared to the top of the wine world thanks to the perfumed, fragrant, full-flavored red winesmade to varying degrees from the Syrah grape. The region is divided into the Northern Rhône, home to several majestic but small appellations, and the Southern Rhône, larger and known for Châteauneuf-du-Pape.

CÔTE ROTIE: The red wines from the Côte Rôtie, or "roasted slopes," reflect the richness and warmth of the area. Smelling of cassis, berries and wildflowers, the wines are great companions to highly seasoned foods and can age for several decades. The leading producers of this splendid wine are Guigal, Jaboulet, Rostaing, Jasmin, Châpoutier and Drevron.

HERMITAGE: Called the "manliest red wine of France," Hermitage is indeed a muscular wine that many connoisseurs rank among the greatest. Though some white wine is made, the reds are in demand, especially those by Paul Jaboulet (La Chapelle), Chave, Châpoutier, Guigal and Sorrel.

CORNAS: A small, 230-acre appellation, Cornas can be a great, less expensive alternative to Hermitage. In outstanding vintages, Cornas competes with its Rhône neighbors and delights its followers. Highly recommmended are Marcel Juge, Auguste Clape and Jaboulet.

CHÂTEAUNEUF-DU-PAPE: Wonderfully diverse and often exciting, Southern Rhône wines are a blend of Grenache, Syrah and eleven other possibilities. The best wines are soft and generous, with an inviting strawberry, spicy, peppery character. After Beaujolais, Châteauneuf-du-Pape is the most versatile food companion. Leaders are Vieux Télégraphe and Beaucastel; Guigal, Fortia, Deydier, Paul Jaboulet, Mont-Olivet, Pignan-Château Reyas, Font du Michelle, Roquette and Mont Redon are also excellent.

CONDRIEU: Almost legendary, Condrieu is a small appellation that yields magnificent white wines. It also contains a seven-acre independent appellation that is so famous the wines are identified by its one producer, Château Grillet. The Condrieu white grape is the Viognier, which imparts an aroma of honeysuckle and ripe pears, with hints of honey and wildflowers. Condrieu is a massive white wine capable of aging for five to eight years. The following are available in the United States: Georges Vernay, Delas Frères, Etienne Guigal and du Rozay.

CHATEAU GRILLET: Made from 100 percent Viognier, this wine from the smallest registered appellation in the world became famous because it was so scarce. Today, it is still wonderful in some vintages. ∎

The Raymonds: Roy Jr., Craig, Benjamin, Walt, Roy Sr.

Heritage,

Dedication,

&

Wines of Distinction

EVEN THOUGH ITS SOILS ARE POOR, THE beautiful Burgundy wine region produces great wines. The famous vineyards climb steep slopes rich in chalk and limestone. Known as the "Côte d'Or," these slopes consist of the Côte de Nuits in the north and the Côte de Beaune in the south, where Pinot Noir is coaxed into fabled red wines and Chardonnay into treasured whites. Vintages vary in quality, especially for reds, and most Burgundies are in short supply.

## WHITE BURGUNDY

CHABLIS: Though the name "Chablis" appears on wines made elsewhere, Chablis itself is a cozy village that produces only white wines from Chardonnay. Quality Chablis is soft in texture yet brisk in acidity, with an aroma of apples and minerals and a hint of butter in the background. The wines are identified by four appellations, which, in descending order of prestige, are Grand Cru, Premier Cru, Chablis and Petit Chablis. The virtues of Chablis are most evident in Grand Cru and Premier Cru. Names with a proven record are Domaine Laroche, William Fèvre, Dauvissat, Raveneau, Baron Patrick, Simmonet-Fèbre and Robert Vocoret.

MEURSAULT: By Burgundy's standards, Meursault is a large region. Best known for its white wines labeled Meursault or Meursault Premier Cru, the region produces a wine with a clovelike spice flavor and a lemony, fruity background. The wines are solid, medium- to full-bodied with lively acidity. The best age for a decade or more. Producers include Comtes Lafon, Louis Jadot, François Jobard, Michelot, J. Matrot and Leroy.

MONTRACHET: Tiny Montrachet became so famous that its two villages, Puligny and Chassagne, changed their names to Puligny-Montrachet and Chassagne-Montrachet. Chassagne-Montrachet and its Premier Cru namesakes are characteristically soft and buttery smooth. Puligny-Montrachet and its Premier Crus are bigger and bolder. Both are top-ranked white wines for aging ability, with those simply called "Montrachet" heading the list. For first-class Puligny-Montrachet, look for vintages from Louis Latour, Leroy, Louis Jadot, Bouchard (Domaine de Château de Beaune), Domaine Leflaive, Michel Colin, Joseph Drouhin and Olivier Leflaive. Chassagne-Montrachet leaders are Bachelet-Ramonet, Marquis de Laguiche, Louis Latour, F. Coffinet, B. Morey, Domaine Duc de Magenta, Joseph Drouhin and Delagrange.

ALOXE CORTON: This simple village is home to what many maintain is the greatest, longest-lived white burgundy of all, Corton-Charlemagne. The wines are honeyed, spicy and exotically scented, with enough depth to justify the expense. Louis Latour's version is often exquisite, as are those by Faiveley, Tollot-Beaut & Fils and Domaine Bonneau de Martray.

## RED BURGUNDY

GEVREY-CHAMBERTIN: This tiny village claims two of the world's most collectible reds, Chambertin and Chambertin Clos de Bez, both of Grand Cru status. Here, the Pinot Noir grape reveals its plum and cherry fragrance in a solid, medium-bodied package. Producers maintaining the region's highest standards include Latour, Faiveley, Joseph Drouhin, Ponsot, Rossignol, Leclerc, Jadot, Mugneret and Grivelet.

MOREY-SAINT-DENIS: Morey-Saint-Denis makes several famous wines, among them the single-vineyard wines of "Clos de Tart," "Clos de Lambrays," "Clos Saint Denis," "Clos de la Roche" and "Bonnes Mares." Characterized by a peppery, earthy component, they have a wonderful velvety texture. Present leaders include the fabled Comte de Vogüé, Domaine Dujac, Domaine Ponsot, Drouhin and Faiveley.

CHAMBOLLE MUSIGNY: At their best, wines from this village are considered to be the most delicate, silky and subtle of all fine red Burgundy. The two famous single vineyards are "Musigny" and "Bonnes Mares." Currently upholding the standards are Comte de Vogüé, Daniel Rion, Jadot, Georges Mugneret, Château de Chambolle-Musigny and Roumier.

ECHÉZEAUX: If this town's name were easier for English-speakers to pronounce, its wines would be better known and higher priced. The Pinot Noir develops plummy fruit and complexity, and the best wines mature early. Look for Drouhin, Georges Mugneret and Bichot.

VOSNE-ROMANÉE: This village would be better known if it were not dominated by one producer, the Domaine de la Romanée Conti. Within the village are seven Grand Cru wines: La Romanée, La Romanée-Conti, La Tâche, Richebourg, Romanée-Saint Vivant, Echézeaux and Grand-Echézeaux. The Grand Crus do not have to reveal which village they call home, which explains why Vosne Romanée remains a sleeper. However, wines identified as Vosne Romanée from the following producers should not disappoint: Meo-Camuzet, Jean Gros, Henri Jayer, Bouchard Père et Fils, Georges Mugneret and Jean Grivot.

VOLNAY: Volnay delivers good-to-exciting red wines to enjoy this decade. The pacesetters are the Domaine des Comtes Lafon, Bouchard Père et Fils (Domaine de Château de Beaune), Domaine de la Pousse d'Or, Michel Lafarge and Domaine Marquis d'Angerville. ∎

# Impeccable Burgundies
## *Since 1859*

# MAISON LOUIS JADOT

IN THE NORTHEAST CORNER OF FRANCE, Champagne is the coolest wine region and has a late, often difficult harvest. Blended from three grapes, Chardonnay, Pinot Noir and Pinot Meunier, Champagne ages in the bottle along with the yeast cells that help develop its complex character. ♦ Champagne's degree of yeasty-toasty character, body (or weight) and relative dryness varies from producer to producer. Each strives for individuality — a "house style." When the wine is properly chilled, Champagne bubbles should be tiny but very active. ♦ Champagnes are also more compatible with meals than once thought, but one must sample a range to find the perfect match. "Brut" is a popular style that's generally not sweet; "extra dry" is sweeter than Brut. ♦ Sparklings, by definition, are wines that have undergone a second fermentation that makes them froth when poured. Winemakers in Southern France noticed that in the spring and fall their wines would get fizzy naturally because of climate changes, and they enjoyed the results. Their efforts to trigger this process became what is today known as the *méthode champenoise*. Almost all viticultural regions in France produce sparkling wines, many by the traditional method. The nearly Champagne *méthode gaillaçoise* and *méthode rural* are also used.

## CHAMPAGNES

NON-VINTAGE BRUT: The majority of Champagne is non-vintage, meaning a blend of wines made in two or more years. The master blend, known as the cuvée, is aged an average of three years, ready to be enjoyed by consumers without additional aging. Like all fine Champagne, it is best served chilled in a tulip or flute-shaped glass. The leading names in the Brut category are Krug, Moët et Chandon, Piper Heidsieck, Laurent Perrier, Bollinger Special Cuvée, Charles Heidsieck Reserve, Veuve Clicquot, Gosset, Mumm Cordon Rouge, Pol Roger, Roederer, Taittinger and Perrier-Jouët.

VINTAGE BRUT: Produced in small quantities, Vintage Champagne generates the most excitement. Made only in the occasional outstanding vintage, it is then given extraspecial aging (five years or more) by the producer. The best represent the highest sensory reward mere grapes can bestow. Among the many fine Vintage Champagnes are those made by Krug, Bollinger "Grand Année," Clicquot "La Grande Dame," Mumm "René Lalou," Perrier-Jouët "Fleur de Champagne," Laurent Perrier "Grand Siècle," Piper Heidsieck "Rare," Philipponnat "Clos des Goisses," Cristal, and the granddaddy of them all, Dom Pérignon.

ROSÉ CHAMPAGNE: Whether vintage or not, Rosé Champagne became the hit bubbly of the 1980s. The delightful russet-pink tint emanates from greater use of red grapes in the cuvée. Most Rosés offer more depth of flavor and a richer body than other Champagnes. As a result, they can be enjoyed with many entrées as well as appetizers. More and more producers are adding a Rosé to their line. The ones to try are Dom Pérignon, Krug, Clicquot, Billecart-Salmon, Bollinger "Grande Année Rosé" and Taittinger "Comtes des Champagnes."

## SPARKLING WINES

### THE LOIRE VALLEY

SAUMUR MOUSSEUX: This appellation near the western end of the Loire Valley, produces some of France's finest and best-known champagne-method sparkling wines. This is in part due to the similarity of the area's soils, extremely high in chalk and limestone, with those of Champagne. Wines under the Samur appelation are produced from 100% Chenin Blanc grapes, the basis of most of the western Loire's sparkling wines. Bouvet-Ladubay makes one of the most elegant and best known sparkling Saumurs, as well as a dry, fruity sparkling rosé and two superb vintage-dated blends, Bouvet Saphir and Bouvet Trésor.

### LANGUEDOC-ROUSSILLON

BLANQUETTE DE LIMOUX: Located amoung southwest France's extensive vineyards, Blanquette de Limoux is the only sparkling wine of the region made by the classic champagne method. The wines are composed pricipally of the Mauzac grape, with some Chenin Blanc and Chardonnay also used.

### THE RHÔNE VALLEY

CLAIRETTE DE DIE: This wine, produced both in still and sparkling versions, takes its name from the Clairette grape on which it is based, an ancient variety first planted in the Rhône Valley by the Romans. The applellation covers 32 villages in the Côte du Rhône, and depending on the production method, may contain one quarter to one half Muscat grapes in the blend. Delightfully perfumed, these refresheing wines are best when drunk young and fresh.

### BURGUNDY

CRÉMANT DE BOURGOGNE : This range of sparkling red, white and rosé wines is made from several traditional Burgundian varieties, including the Chardonnay, the Pinot Noir and the Gamay Noir. The best-known producer is Kriter, and Veuve Amiot and Delorme make excellent wines as well.

# THE BEST KEPT SECRET
## OF
# BAROLO

# BRICCO VIOLE
## by
## SYLLA SEBASTE

Azienda Agricola Sebaste - Località S. Pietro delle Viole - 12060 Barolo (CN) - Italy

# ITALIAN WINES

L IKE THE FRENCH, THE ITALIANS HAVE been making wine longer than anyone else. Over the centuries, Italy perfected its own unique regional varieties and now produces billions of gallons a year. ♦ Many Italian wines, like most French wines, are identified by region, such as Chianti, and the flavors and aromas reflect their growing region and climate. Appellation of origin is emphasized and, although it does not promise quality, it *does* guarantee authenticity. Since appellation is so important, the use of place names is strictly controlled by the Italian government. The year the grapes were picked and made into wine is another important factor. ♦ Italian grapes are sometimes planted on difficult sites causing quality and taste variations from year to year. The best solution: let the great vintages age; drink the lesser vintages young.

TRENTINO-
ALTO ADIGE

Milan

Turin

FRIULI

PIEDMONT

Venice

Genoa

Florence

TUSCANY

MONTALCINO

Rome

ITALY

VITICULTURAL

AREAS

Palermo

# THE BEST KEPT SECRET
## OF
# MONFERRATO

# MIMOSA
## by
## COLLE MANORA

Azienda Agricola Manora - Via Bozzole 4 - 15044 Quargnento (AL) - Italy

## FROM THE PIEDMONT DISTRICT SOUTH OF

Alba comes one of the world's most powerful and long-lived red wines, Barolo. Historians call Barolo the "wine of kings, and the king of wines." It takes its name from the village of Barolo and is made from the Nebbiolo variety, a highly sensitive grape that develops well along the hillsides. Barolo has enchanting, contrasting aromas of truffles and roses, tar and spices. An acquired taste, fine Barolo is big, robust and strong in alcohol, with a degree of woodiness after long aging. Like many great wines, it is made in small quantities: only 3,000 acres comprise the delimited area. The Nebbiolo makes many other red wines in neighboring sectors of Piedmont, and they too are presented here.

**BAROLO:** To qualify for the name, a Barolo must be given at least three years of aging, two in barrel. A Barolo Riserva is aged for a minimum of five years, two in barrel, before it is sold. A Riserva often needs years, even decades, of aging to reach its prime. Among the leaders are Ceretto, Aldo Conterno, Giacosa, Vietti, Prunotto, Pio Cesare, Mascarello and Fontanafredda. Today, the most exciting Barolos are the single-vineyard versions, especially those by Ceretto called "Bricco Rocche" and "Prapo Bricco Rocche."

**BARBARESCO:** Just east of Alba, the town of Barbaresco is well regarded for its red wine made from Nebbiolo. The regular bottlings are aged at least two years, and the Riservas must be held for four. The single-vineyard wines from Gaja called "Sori Tildin" and "Sori San Lorenzo" are remarkable. "Bricco Asili" is the outstanding wine from Ceretto. Other worthwhile Barbarescos are Prunotto, "Asij" from Ceretto, Castello di Neive and Bruno Giacosa, especially his "Santo Stefano de Neive Riserva."

**DOLCETTO:** "Dolcetto" means sweet, but this Piedmont wine is medium-bodied and dry. The best versions offer an exquisite aroma of strawberries and cherries, with a refreshing acidity and moderate tannins. One of the finest is by Marcarini, with its "Bioschi di Berri" special batch made from ancient vines. Other first-rate producers are Giacosa, Mascarello, Clerico, Vietti and Bel Colle.

**NEBBIOLO D'ALBA:** Similar to Barbaresco, Nebbiolo d'Alba is somewhat more variable in quality. Originating from vineyards surrounding Alba that are outside of both Barolo and Barbaresco, it reaches maturity sooner than Barolo, yet still offers richness and complexity. Leading producers include Angelo Gaja, Bruno Giacosa, Scarpa, Alfredo Prunotto, Fontanafredda, Mascarello and Ceretto. ∎

**BRUNELLO, SAID TO BE A SPECIAL VARIANT** of Sangiovese, the Chianti grape, flourishes in the village of Montalcino in southern Tuscany. This rich and long-lived wine is famous thanks to the Biondi-Santi family, developers of the special grape in the 1880s and for years the only major producer. Other companies have developed vineyards around Montalcino, including Banfi with its magnificent Castello Banfi, and just over 2,000 acres are now planted. ♦ The regulations governing Brunello production state that it must be given a minimum of four years' aging prior to release, and it must be barrel- or wood-aged for three and a half. An alternative designation, Rosso di Montalcino, was established for wines that were not aged in wood for any set minimum. Of late, these fruitier wines have found a niche in the market.

**BRUNELLO DI MONTALCINO:** Powerful and compact, Brunello wines offer berries and spice along with leathery, earthy components. They can be extremely astringent when young and need cellaring for at least ten years. Biondi-Santi reigns supreme, but the competition includes Banfi, San Felice, Col d'Orcia, Il Greppone Mazzi and Caparzo.

**ROSSO DI MONTALCINO:** Some Americans prefer this to Brunello. The plummy fruit and richness is unencumbered by wood, but there's plenty of tannin for aging at least five years. Both Caparzo and Banfi make excellent versions, as do Col d'Orcia and Biondi-Santi.

**SASSICAIA:** From the outskirts of Tuscany near Bolgheri comes a red wine that enjoys a fanatic cult following, Sassicaia. Made from Cabernet Sauvignon and Cabernet Franc, it is produced by Tenuta San Guido and was among the first Italian wines to resemble a truly first-class Bordeaux.

**AMARONE:** Amarone is a special red wine made near Verona in the Valpolicella district. Incredibly powerful and exotically scented, it is made by selecting very ripe grapes that are dried on trays for three months to concentrate their flavor. The wine is not actually made until late January of the following year. Masi offers classic Amarone. ∎

**TAURASI:** An extraordinary wine that seems to age for decades, Taurasi is made from an ancient grape variety, the Aglianico. It responds magically to the conditions in and around Avelino, which is in the south in Campania. The village of Taurasi is represented by the Mastroberardinos, a great wine-producing family. ∎

ONE OF THE OLDEST AND BEST-KNOWN wines, Chianti has recently been in a state of flux. The leaders in Tuscany are redesigning their famous wine, hoping to bury its image as a cheap carafe wine in a straw-wrapped bottle. In 1984, they took the first step and changed the regulations to allow producers to use better-suited grapes and more red than white varieties. ♦ Chianti is already new and improved, and since the Tuscan hills yield around ten million cases annually, there's plenty to go around.

CHIANTI: Wine simply labeled "Chianti" tends to be the lightest in style. Intended to be enjoyed in its youth, this style of Chianti is the most popular wine in the many fine restaurants of Florence. Several well-established producers do send some here, including the leaders, Frescabaldi and Barone Ricasoli, as well as Rampolla, Gabbiano and Pasolini.

CHIANTI CLASSICO: This designation applies to wines produced in the official "inner zone" between Siena and Florence. Typically full-flavored yet balanced, Classico wines have berries, spice and an occasional leathery component in the aroma. To protect the region's reputation, producers formed an association that uses the black rooster as its symbol. About one-third of all Chianti is Classico, and the greatest improvements are apparent in its bottlings. Among the best are Antinori, Castello del Rampolla, Isole E Olena, Lilliano, Castello di Volpaia and Villa Caffaggio.

CHIANTI CLASSICO RISERVA: When the wines are aged three years or more by the producer, they earn the designation "Riserva." Aging can be either in barrels or bottles, so the style of the final wine varies widely. Usually the pride of the house, Riservas are the best Chiantis for aging. "Ducale" from Ruffino is famous, as are Antinori's and Villa Banfi's. Others to look for are Isole E Olena, Il Paggio, Castello di Abolo, Castello del Rampolla, Castello di Querceto, San Felice, Monsanto, Cispiano, Melini, Nozzole, La Massa, Ricasoli Fossi and Il Poggiolino.

VINO DA TAVOLA: This lowly sounding designation means "table wine," but it often appears on wines that are creative and profoundly exciting. Part of the new wave of Italian reds, they are usually produced in Tuscany and Piedmont, using grapes and combinations not permitted for their appellations but capable of greatness nonetheless. Unable to label them by their place names, producers create proprietary names, such as Antinori's 1971 renegade blend, Tignanello. Other new-wave, truly exciting reds to look for are Solaia (Antinori), Campofiorin (Masi), Tinscvil (Monsanto), Cabreo (Ruffino), Vigorello (San Felice) and Sammarco (di Rampolla). ■

UPGRADING ITALIAN WHITE WINES TO MAKE to make them equal to the reds while appealing to current taste preferences has demanded a recent outpouring of money and effort. Once-proud vineyards are switching to such varieties as Chardonnay and Sauvignon Blanc, while old-fashioned white grapes such as Trebbiano are disappearing. The new-wave Italian whites have varietal designations that simplify marketing — sometimes the special blends even carry made-up proprietary names. Today, two regions enjoying particular success with white wines are located in the north: Trentino-Alto Adige and Friuli. Other new-wave whites are coming from Tuscany and Piedmont.

PINOT GRIGIO: A pleasantly fruity, spicy white wine, Pinot Grigio is coming into its own. It is medium- to light-bodied with good, snappy acidity. Some of the best producers include Brigil in the Alto Adige, Boscaini, Plozner, La Viarte and Tieffenbrunner. Banfi subtitles its lovely Pinot Grigio "San Angelo."

ARNEIS: Made in Piedmont from Arneis grapes, this is a distinctive light, fruity wine with a slight spritz. Two important producers are Ceretto ("Blange") and Giacosa.

CHARDONNAY: Because Italian vintners want to show their oenological abilities to the world, they are working to style Chardonnay like a Meursault or a Napa Valley barrel-aged version. Among the pioneers are Gaja's full-bodied Chardonnay from Piedmont, Banfi's impressive "Fontanelle," and Santa Margarita, with vineyards in Alto Adige. Another major player is Avbignone's "Il Marzocco."

ORVIETO: From Umbria comes Orvieto, a blend of several varieties. Uneven in quality until the early 1980s, it has been coming on strong in recent years. The most consistent are those labeled "Classico." Quality-minded producers include Barbi, Antinori, Barberani, Bigi and Melini.

SOAVE: As the most popular white export, Soave can make a pleasant companion. Several producers in Veneto are working hard to give it more character. They include Pieropan, Anselmi and Masi.

PROPRIETARY WHITES: The ubiquitous Antinori family makes the lovely "Galestro," a blend of Sauvignon Blanc and Procanico. "Libaio" is a terrific white wine from the house of Ruffino that blends Chardonnay with Sauvignon Blanc. Introduced by Brolio Ricasoli, "Nebbiano" is a lovely, lively white wine made from Sauvignon Blanc and the Italian Riesling. "Terre Alte" from Livio Felluga is a classic white wine blended from Toscai, Sauvignon Blanc and Pinot Blanco grapes. ■

**Norman Roby** *is director of the Academy of Wine in Mendocino and a columnist for* The Wine Spectator

# MOLTO
*STILE*
*QUALITÀ*
*MODERNO*
*ITALIANO*

# CERETTO

**CERETTO**
Produce ed affina vini del Piemonte in Alba
BARBARESCO
Denominazione di origine controllata
e garantita

ETICHETTE DISEGNATE DA *SILVIO COPPOLA*, MILANO

Imported by International Vintage Wine Co., Hartford Ct.

Registro imbott. 8671 CN - Imbott

# IF ITS LEGENDARY IMAGE DOESN'T TEMPT YOU, SURELY THE RICHNESS OF ITS FLAVOR AND AROMA WILL

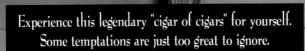

Experience this legendary "cigar of cigars" for yourself.
Some temptations are just too great to ignore.

THE BEST OF

## CIGARS

BY RICHARD L. DI MEOLA

# CIGAR SMOKING ENJOYS A RENAISSANCE

MARK TWAIN, A TRUE cigar lover, once said, "If I cannot smoke in heaven, I shall not go!"

Today, many people share the same opinion. Although it is certainly not a necessity, cigar smoking can be one of life's special pleasures. The aroma, ritual and draw, along with the feel of the cigar in one's mouth, comprise a total, satisfying experience.

Combined with an after-dinner libation, a fine cigar is the ultimate cap to a fine dinner. The smoker can sit back, relax and linger while the plates are cleared and the conversation mellows. Yet cigar lovers do not always wait for the evening meal to indulge in their passion. Many men enjoy a good smoke in the morning, perhaps an hour after breakfast. At this time of day, the cigar is no longer an extension of a repast. Instead it helps the smoker transcend his surroundings, giving him a moment to pause and reflect upon his activities and perhaps feel less hectic about them.

Lunch, too, is a favorite time for cigar smoking. The experience is different than the evening meal because it's generally without a complementary drink and the taste and aroma are a wonderful segue into the rest of the day. Usually light cigars are smoked by day, heavier ones at night.

Although there are no rules about when to smoke, there are often restrictions on where to smoke. Some restaurants encourage patrons to enjoy an after-dinner smoke, while others cater to the wishes of their non-smoking guests. Getting to know which restaurants are cigar friendly is one way to ensure a pleasant experience for all. Lately, though, interest in good cigars is enjoying a renaissance. Positive publicity about cigars has contributed to this, much of it from restaurants, hotels and clubs. All over America, these establishments have been conducting private

© 1993 Cifuentes y Cia

**The cigar that knew Cuba when.**
Only Partagas cigars are
handmade by Ramon Cifuentes,
the same man who made them over
40 years ago in Havana.

# PARTAGAS®

IN THE GREAT CUBAN TRADITION

smoker dinners that resemble legal speakeasies. From barbecue to black-tie, from $25 to $250 (there was a $1,000-a-plate charity smoker in New York not long ago), these affairs offer men, and women so inclined, the chance to gather over a meal and smoke cigars to their hearts' content.

About 400 such events take place a year. As a result, many fine restaurants have created separate, permanent smoking rooms and humidors are making a comeback. The main dining room is usually off-limits, but, more and more, smokers can adjourn to an adjoining lounge.

Not only that, but the $5 and $10 stogie is in great demand. It seems a more expensive cigar appeals to the psyche of some aficionados, just as an expensive watch appeals to its owner, yet there are some wonderful, inexpensive cigars available if the smoker does a little homework.

Typically, novices begin smoking cigars at the age of 35, although today they often begin a bit younger. They start as occasional smokers, for celebrations or during special events, and usually purchase more expensive cigars at the beginning. As the beauty and pleasure of smoking become apparent, they start indulging in a smoke alone. Next, they get to know a good tobacconist and explore the myriad of lower-priced cigars in the shop. Soon they are smoking cigars frequently and for less money.

Things get interesting when the smoker is more experienced. Exploring the multitude of blends, wrapper colors and sizes available and becoming conversant in cigars means the smoker is on the road to becoming an aficionado, a cigar lover who smokes six a week. At this point, smokers generally go back to smoking more expensive cigars.

## THE ORIGINS OF FINE CIGARS

The $10 cigars available in America today are most likely rolled in the Dominican Republic, Honduras, Jamaica or Mexico. There are others that come from the Canary Islands, Panama, Costa Rica and Nicaragua, but

Dominican and Honduran cigars together make up 80% of the premium cigar market in the United States.

Cuban cigars are still illegal, but even before the Cuban embargo more than thirty years ago, cigars actually made in Cuba never accounted for more than 9% of the premium American market. That was when the most popular price category for the best cigars, Cuban or "Clear Havana," was 35 cents for a Corona shape, 42 ring by 5 1/2 inch length. (In America, a cigar's girth is measured by "ring" size, one ring being equivalent to 1/64th inch or a bit more than 5/8 of an inch.)

In the 1950s, more expensive, larger cigars sold for 65 to 70 cents. Clear Havana cigars were those made of 100% Havana tobacco, but rolled in the United States. All the best were made by hand, as the best Caribbean and Central American cigars are today. Thirty years ago, even lesser cigars contained some Havana tobacco because it was considered unparalleled in the world. In other words, in those days the important thing was not that cigars were rolled in Cuba, although 91% of the best were, but that the tobacco was Cuban.

Now we have excellent tobacco growing in Central American, Brazil, Cameroon, Mexico, Indonesia and other places. Expert Cuban growers are no longer in Cuba today because they fled the country with their seeds which they planted, cultivated and nurtured in the countries mentioned above. They are now producing the finest, tastiest, most aromatic cigar tobaccos the world has ever known.

Sadly, the Cuban economy has slipped dramatically over the years, and fertilizers, insecticides and even expertise are scarce. As a result, the cigars being produced outside of Cuba today and regularly offered in the United States are the most superior. When Cuba finally rejoins the democratic community and the embargo is lifted, there will be renewed interest in Cuban cigars and tobacco. Cigar manufacturers will want to experiment with the blends they so painstakingly evolved over thirty years and bring new tastes, aromas and nuance to them by mixing in Cuban tobacco. But improving the current crop conditions in Cuba will take many years.

## CIGARS

## WRAPPERS

The tobacco used in brands available in America is the most expensive in the world. Wrapper tobacco, the half leaf wrapped around the outside of the cigar, the one the smoker sees and feels, is the most expensive, cultivated for eye appeal and smoothness to the touch. It is, after all, the part of the cigar that caresses its owner's lips.

One of the varieties most widely used is the Connecticut Shade Grown, grown in Connecticut. It is allowed to sprout and mature under constructed layers of cheesecloth to protect it from the sun. The resulting leaf stays relatively light in color, although various shades of brown are yielded. The veins are acceptable, and the leaves are large and smooth. This tobacco presents the smoker with a perfect first impression. Lightness and smoothness portend mildness and a graceful taste. The best of this tobacco costs $40 per pound compared with many other types at $10 per pound.

Another popular wrapper is grown in Cameroon and Central Africa. This is Sun-Grown leaf, allowed to mature on the stalk without protection. It is a bit sandy and dark brown in color. Cameroon wrapper is sweeter and more aromatic than Connecticut Shade.

Like food connoisseurs, most cigar aficionados "taste" with their eyes. While this is good, it is also important to enjoy the cigar for what it is, stripped of any visual cues.

Consider the Maduro wrapper. It is black and looks strong, even harsh. The best Maduro wrappers come from Mexico and Connecticut. Known as Connecticut Broadleaf, the Connecticut version is a heavy, veiny tobacco rich in oils, much like its Mexican relative. Dark to begin with, the tobacco when treated with heat and steam turns jet black. Before lighting up, one might think this cigar would be too harsh to enjoy, but this is not so. Properly treated, blended and rolled, Maduro wrapped cigars are often the sweetest and richest of all for those with an acquired taste.

Indonesian Java and Sumatra are good wrapper tobaccos that lend their own characteristics to the cigars they cover, as are the wrappers of Honduras, Ecuador and Nicaragua.

## BINDERS & FILLERS

The binder is another half leaf. It is rolled around the filler, forming what is called the "bunch." The binder's role is to hold the filler together so that the bunch can be presented to the wrapper for covering. It can affect the cigar's taste and aroma, so it must be carefully chosen, although the purpose of its heavy leaf is strength. The best binder in the world is Santo Domingo from the Dominican Republic. Mexican is a close second. Java third. If a manufacturer wants to add a nuance of taste and aroma, Java, Cameroon or even Connecticut might be used.

The filler in a fine, premium cigar is its soul. Never to be chopped up, as in inexpensive cigars, the leaves are folded into the cigar whole after being stripped of two-thirds of their center stems. In this condition, after preparation, they are called "frog strips," because the remainders of the leaves after stripping resemble dangling frogs legs. It is with these tobaccos that the cigar manufacturer can get creative and with them that growers have had success in cultivating magnificent strains of leaf.

The filler tobacco grown from Cuban seed in the Dominican Republic is called Piloto Cubano. It is rich, zesty and spicy tobacco. There are a couple of categories,"Seco" and "Ligero," and within each category, six to eight sub-types. Smart manufacturers know what each category and sub-type will bring to a blend and they experiment with them to create subtleties of taste and aroma.

There are also filler tobaccos grown from "home" seed in the Dominican Republic, Mexico, Java, Brazil, Honduras and other countries, each with their own unique characteristics. Deciphering the best ways to use these traits in blends takes years of experience. Even after a manufacturer has the knowledge, blending filler tobaccos, combining them with a binder and finishing the cigar with the proper wrapper is something like getting the tumblers of a lock to fall into place without knowing the combination.

187

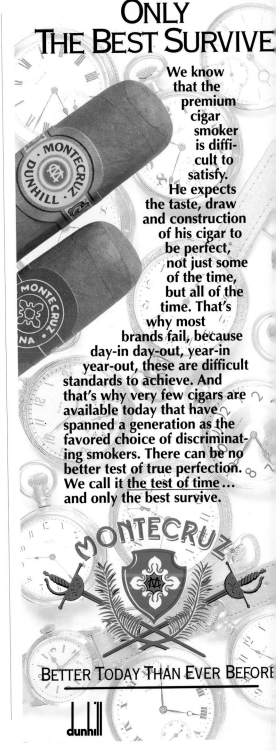

For the smoker, all the different brands and blends on the market make the task of finding what tastes best a similar mystique, but one that is fun, rewarding and indescribably pleasurable when discovered.

## PUTTING IT ALL TOGETHER

Knowing the characteristics of tobaccos for blending is not enough. It is equally important to know how to roll. If the cigar is not properly constructed, it will not smoke well and the taste and aroma will be seriously flawed. The only way to make a fine cigar is by hand. No machine can "feel" the density of long filler along the length. The chopped up tobacco in short-filled cigars burns fast and hot, and such cigars do not hold their ash. Only those using frog-stripped filler leaves, folded together into their binders with skill, will burn slowly, evenly and cool.

Only a well-made cigar allows the blended leaf to deliver full richness of flavor. Flavor and aroma in cigars are described by those who make them with words like aromatic, sweet, zesty, peppery, piquant, pungent, floral, earthy, rich, full, light, grassy, woody and when the description isn't flattering, bitter, strong, harsh, astringent, dirty, acidic, ammoniacal.

The most frequent construction flaw in a cigar is hard draw. The most frustrating thing in the world for a cigar lover is to pay good money for a cigar and find that the smoke won't come out. Finding a knowledgeable tobacconist one can trust, preferably an avid cigar smoker, can help avoid this dilemma. Only after building up trust in the consistency of a cigar brand can the smoker label the brand a "good cigar."

The size of the cigar also makes a big difference in the delivery of taste and aroma. The 48 ring, 3/4 diameter has sufficient long filler to enable the manufacturer to be creative in his combinations. It also delivers a greater volume of smoke and richness. Thinner brands have fewer leaves in the blend and are therefore more simple, less complex. It is also more difficult to make the thinner brands by hand so the chance of getting one that doesn't burn properly is greater.

Cigar smokers usually experiment until they find the size suitable to their individual taste and usually stick to it. If a smoker is looking for a favorite-sized cigar in a favorite brand and doesn't find it, chances are the smoker will select the same, tried-and-true size in another brand rather than make another size selection within the same brand.

When a great cigar is produced, it is crucial that it is kept in proper condition. A dry cigar will not be a good cigar, no matter how perfect it was when it left the manufacturer. It will smoke harsh and the wrapper is likely to unravel. Good merchants, therefore, religiously keep their stock in proper humidity. The smoker should, too. A humidor with a properly charged humidifier is the proper way to store cigars. The humidistat should always be pointed to "wet."

The enjoyment of fine cigars is a unique pleasure. It can be ritualistic or simple, whether the head of the cigar is opened with a gold cutter or the pinch of fingernails. The end that is lit, the tuck, is lit first before being placed in the mouth. Then the flame of a second match dances below the end of the cigar while drawing and twirling until the cigar is fully alight, ready to fulfill the smoker's expectation of spirited, spicy and aromatic richness.

There aren't any fast rules for smoking fine cigars other than considerate etiquette and common sense. Dining in restaurants where cigar smoking is welcomed doesn't mean ignoring nearby tables with guests in the middle of a meal. Adjourning to the lounge is still the right thing to do. On the other hand, in prohibitive restaurants, it is often possible to enjoy a cigar, after asking, when the establishment is not very full.

All cigar lovers should stay aware and practice smoking etiquette, and find the cigar of his, or her, dreams. ∎

---

**Richard Di Meola** *is the*
*Executive Vice President, Chief Operating Officer of*
*Consolidated Cigar Corp. and a cigar lover.*

| Los Angeles | Orange County |
|---|---|
| Beau Rivage | Antoine |
| Bernard's | Bistango |
| Bikini | The Cellar |
| Bistro 45 | The Club Grill & Bar |
| Bistro Garden | The Dining Room |
| Bistro Garden at Coldwater | The Golden Truffle |
| Cafe La Boheme | La Vie en Rose |
| Campanile | Mr. Stox |
| Chasen's | The Ritz |
| Chinois on Main | Trees |
| The Chronicle | |
| Cicada | *San Diego Area* |
| Citrus | El Bizcocho |
| Drago | Mille Fleurs |
| Emporio Armani Express | *Santa Barbara* |
| Fennel | El Encanto |
| Fresco Ristorante | Wine Cask |
| I Cugini | |
| La Chaumiere | |
| L'Escoffier | |
| L'Opera | |
| L'Orangerie | |
| Lunaria | |
| Ma Maison | |
| McCormick & Schmick's | |
| Opus | |
| Orleans | |
| Parkway Grill | |
| Fennel | |
| Remi | |
| Rockenwagner | |
| Trader Vic's | |
| Tryst | |
| Tuttobene | |
| Xiomara | |

# "Agnes, have you seen my Don Diegos?"

We're so sure you'll love today's Don Diego Cigars we'll give you a sample box of ten Petit Coronas, 5 1/8" x 42 ring, (a $20.00 value) for five dollars cash or check. Write Don Diego, P.O. Box 24146ER, Richmond, VA 23224. Offer not available to minors. Offer expires December 31, 1994. Limit one per customer.

# EPICUREAN RENDEZVOUS

*gratefully acknowledges the support*
*of the following sponsors*

# RESTAURANT INDEX

## LOS ANGELES AREA

## ORANGE COUNTY

## SAN DIEGO AREA

## SANTA BARBARA

## CUISINE KEY

| | |
|---|---|
| AMR = American | ITA = Italian |
| CAL = California | JPN = Japanese |
| CAR = Caribbean | MED = Mediterranean |
| CHI = Chinese | POL = Polynesian |
| CON = Continental | SEA = Seafood |
| FRN = French | SWE = Swedish |
| INT = International | SWS = Southwestern |